naked vinyl

Tim O'Brien & Mike Savage

naked vinyl

Classic Nude Album Cover Art

Chrysalis
Impact

First published in 2002 by Chrysalis Impact,
An imprint of Chrysalis Books plc
64, Brewery Road,
London N7 9NT
United Kingdom

ISBN 1 84411 005 2

Credits
Commissioning Editors: Will Steeds, Chris Stone
Editors: Chris Westhorp, Jo Richardson
Designed by Grade Design Consultants, London; Jacket design: Christine Taylor
Production: David Proffit and Beth Sweeney
Colour reproduction: Anorax Imaging Ltd
Printed and bound in Spain

Record label credits
ABC/Paramount: pg 41; Audio Fidelity: 45, 47, 141; BAF: 161; Barclay: 222–223; Beacon: 57, 58; Boulevard: 149, 151;
Capitol/EMI: 12, 28, 30, 33, 233; Carrere: 255; Casablanca: 201; CBS: 158–159; Damont: 167, 169; Davis: 49, 51, 53, 55;
Deacon: 153, 155; Decca: 27, 29, 157, 177, 178–179, 181, 185; Durium: 144, 227, 228, 229, 230, 231, 236, 243, 245, 249;
Elastic: 175; Elektra: 39, 193; EMI (Courtesy of EMI Records Ltd.): 33, 190–191, 239; Essex: 12; Fax: 18, 21, 64, 67, 68–69, 70,
71, 72, 73, 75, 77, 78, 79, 81, 85, 87, 89; Hanover: 129; Joy: 183; Jubilee: 43; Kanrom: 108–109, 110–111, 112, 113, 114–115;
Laff: 93, 95, 97, 99, 101, 103, 104–105, 107; Magnet: 197, 198; Malligator: (Cover of *Cerrone's Paradise* copyright by Malligator
Productions. Photo by Patrick Peroquin, 1977): 205; Marble Arch: 121; Master: 215; Mercury: 34; Mint: 125; Music World: 217,
219, 221; Nems: 209; Normal: 251; Party Pool: 117; Pye: 34, 119; Que: 59, 61; RCA: 10, 11, 165, 172, 189, 213; Request: 133,
135; Select: 127; Shark: 235; Strand: 31, 83; Sunset: 123; T.K.: 192; Treasure: 131; Trend: 170–171; United Artists: 146–147,
190–191; Vedette: 199; V.I.P.: 253; Viking: 139; Virgin: 210–211, 241; Vogue: 203; Young Blood International: 187

Photographic credits
Hulton Getty: 17, 172; Corbis: 91, 173, 194–95, 207, 247, 251.

Contents

About the Authors

Tim O'Brien was born in 1972 in Clapham in South London, England. He grew up in nearby Streatham and was educated at the Ernest Bevin Secondary School in Tooting. After school, he embarked on a wayward trail of pointless adventure, that took him through Bristol, Brighton, New Zealand, and Japan. A seasoned record collector, he settled finally to write and compile *Naked Vinyl*.

Mike Savage was also born in Clapham in 1972, and he grew up there. He, too, attended the Ernest Bevin Secondary School, which was where he bought Tim O'Brien a chocolate bar and a friendship was born. From Tooting he embarked on a trail of debauchery, as equally wayward as his friend's, settling only to found Prime Cuts, a successful Bristol-based record shop.

Foreword

Naked Vinyl was born in Bristol, southwest England.
Bristol has housed much musical talent over the years, from Massive Attack to Portishead, and beyond and the legacy of this local talent is reflected in a depth of musical knowledge and creativity. The city houses some of Britain's best record shops, as well as many of the country's most obsessive record collectors.

It was in this music-loving environment that our two minds pondered over the vinyl record as a product and the range of cover designs that are used to sell it. As we perused the stock of Prime Cuts, we came to realize that, just as there is a song for almost every occasion, so there is also a cover for every season – and within each of the seasons there is a host of vibrant artistic meditations on almost any theme imaginable.

As the days passed – and they can do so slowly in Bristol – our minds ticked over. And an idea slowly began to form, one that brought together nudity and the record to form a beautiful whole. From there on the task was easy: collect the best that this genre has to offer, work out the themes that bind the records together, and complete the erotic beast that you hold here before you.

Naked Vinyl is, of course, the fruit of that labour. It was written and compiled by Tim O'Brien and is from an original idea by Mike Savage and Tim O'Brien; we hope it is a book that brings you as much pleasure as it does us.

Introduction

Naked Fun

Welcome to *Naked Vinyl*, the book that brings together music, art, photography, design, and nudity. Over the next 200-plus pages you will be looking at the best that this newly discovered genre has to offer and we're pretty sure your eyes will have seen little like it before. We've searched high and low to bring you the rudest, most stylish collection of nude covers we could find, so now it's time for you to sit back, relax, and treat your eyes to a feast of flesh in our smorgasbord of smut.

Naked Vinyl is an unashamedly modern affair. Playful, sassy, and fun, the book offers pop art for the music-loving masses and record cover art for the vinyl connoisseur; in the process, it serves as a reminder of times of well-defined, politically incorrect sexual roles. *Naked Vinyl*'s place in the entertainment pantheon is somewhere between the art of Andy Warhol and *Men Only* magazine; it is a book that is yours to treasure in all its light-hearted glory.

The Life and Times of Naked Vinyl

"Naked Vinyl" is essentially "cheesecake" in character.
Cheesecake was born of the desire to entertain American troops in World War II and after the war cheesecake imagery remained a fresh part of culture. Cheesecake imagery was sexy and "from pin-up queens Betty Gable and Rita Hayworth, to the glamour girls painted on the noses of fighter planes, to nude photos passed around the barracks, female pulchritude was considered downright patriotic". This then was the art of cheesecake and in a post-war world that was re-assessing its relationship to sex, it was cheesecake that provided the most ready and prodigious sexual output.

Cheesecake cover art was born in the minds of designers and marketing men seeking to sell records as home entertainment. It began in the late '40s as naked women graced album covers with their nudity imaginatively disguised. These covers were stylishly posed montages of model, scene, and typography and they began a trend that would lead to the fully nude naked vinyl cover.

One favoured gimmick employed by cheesecake cover art was to make a play on the title of the record, a visual pun that let the erotic world slip in subtly, almost unnoticed. In this way, *Wish You Were Here* (right) features a woman alone on an island with only a telescope and her ripped and revealing nightie for company. While *Warm and Tender* (above) features a woman lounging amid home furnishings, her nightdress intact, a glimpse of thigh revealed, and a warm, loving pussycat for company.

This was a time when the subtle erotic image ruled and many beautiful covers were produced that are cherished by collectors to this day.

who left civilization to commune with nature") and bigger budget sex flicks, such as *Thar She Blows*: "filmed in colour aboard a 100-foot twin-screw cruiser". These films came with beautifully designed sexy film posters in tow. Finally, with the success of the big-breasted '60s blockbusters of Russ Meyer, it was clear that sex in the movies was here to stay.

Sex also sold magazines and the success of *Playboy* helped to pave the way for the rise of naked vinyl. In the '50s, *Playboy* gave vent to the desires of the red-blooded American male, and in its trailblazing wake came a wave of copycat magazines and spin-off culture.

Former *Playboy* models, such as June Blair, Dawn Richard, Alice Denham, and Jayne Mansfield, featured on record covers, while the magazine even released the occasional record, such as 1958's *Playboy* jazz-allstars album.

In the same year, *Playboy* magazine featured a pictorial feature about erotic record cover art, using the headline "music to make your eyeballs pop" – and the somewhat cryptic byline "jacket art hath pulchritude to soothe the savage breast". *Playboy* documented the rise of this erotic art thus: "During the last half decade, LP manufacturers did a lot to pep up the product outside as well as in. They called on top-notch artists and designers to turn out genuinely jazzy jacket art that helped sales soar. They also turned to a discovery made by the paperback publishers before them: that a seasoning of sex on covers could jack up the sales curve still higher". In this way pulp fiction, album art, and *Playboy* set the scene for what was to follow.

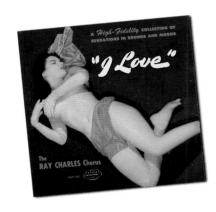

The Art of Cheesecake

Artists such as Les Baxter, Nelson Riddle, Martin Denny, and George Shearing all flirted with the nude cover, remaining just the right side of respectability and safely in the land of cheesecake. Teasing us with a pair of sexy eyes or a little cleavage, the album art of these famous individuals placed smouldering female sexuality delicately on the cover. Record and image combined to produce vinyl portraits; items of stylish ephemera with which to grace living room, cabinet, and stereo alike. Never quite daring enough to risk full-frontal poses, these cheesecake covers made you smile with a sexy, flirtatious *joi de vivre*.

It wasn't long, though, before coy was no longer cool, and whereas cheesecake covers sold love to a world entranced by the romance of Hollywood movies, naked vinyl brought us back down to earth by selling sex to a world demanding its share of the erotic. Sex and society had begun to merge and the scene was set for the full-scale assault of nudity on the eyes, minds, and morals of the Western world.

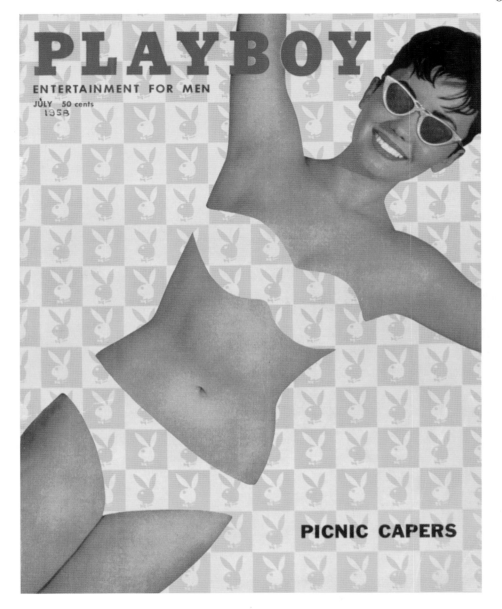

Adam and Eve

Sex was set to make vinyl its next conquest. Within a year, Adam magazine (one of Playboy's more erotic imitators) was featuring articles about stripping alongside nude starlets and, further inside, advertisements for the latest record releases.

Adam magazine was a feast of erotica and in 1960 it ran an article about "the madcap escapades of showgirls", in which it related how Greta Thyssen, a former Miss Denmark, was "posing for a cheesecake photographer when she suddenly remembered that it was the last day she had to register as an alien", thus she slinked, clad in bikini, to the nearest Hollywood mail office, causing chaos along the way. "Shenanigans and wild capers are par for the course in the exciting world of busty beauties", the reader is told, while the model claims she was merely saving time.

Later in the magazine, the Los Angeles nightclub The York is showcased under the headline "the York flips its cork", with pictures of performers, patrons, and strippers featured alongside a biography of owner Bill York. The York was the kind of venue that spawned the comedy, song, and dance that would be featured in the records released by naked vinyl labels.

Adam magazine eventually tapped its own cultural output to release a series of records featuring sexy songs and up-front comedians. The advertisements for these albums tell us about the stars of the records and what we can expect for our hard-earned money. Suitably encouraged, *Adam* magazine urges us to hand over our cash and await delivery.

Nightclubs, comedians, strippers, aspiring actresses, Hollywood, record labels, and magazines all fed off one another to provide income, entertainment, and career enhancement. With many of the record labels based near Hollywood, it was easy for them to feed off a pool of seasoned female performers, and with so many aspiring actresses around, a suitable roster of models and starlets was never far away.

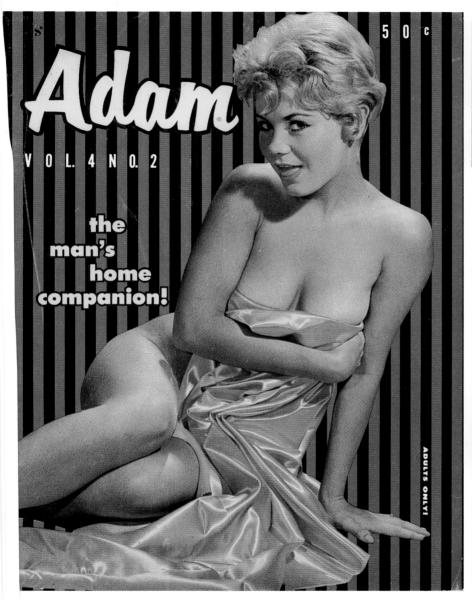

5 0 c

Adam

VOL. 4 NO. 2

the
man's
home
companion!

ADULTS ONLY!

STAG
PARTY
SPECIAL

The Stag Party Record

Naked vinyl really came into its own with the advent of the '60s stag party record. Billed as albums for "bachelors and broad-minded men", these records portrayed the world of sex in all its seedy glory. They were sold as the ideal accompaniment to any such party, though more likely than not they were listened to by the collector, his feet up, drink to hand, and his wife no doubt elsewhere. Down at heel, grubby, and crude, these records sold a fantasy of sexual freedom; an escape from the constricting sexual morality of a none-too-decadent time. Home entertainment would never be the same again. The bachelors and "broad-minded men" (for which read "husbands") were encouraged to live a life of sexual laissez faire by records that uncovered just about every conceivable aspect of sex, from the supposed delights of the Orient to the dangers of the doctor's waiting room.

Stag party records were championed by the aforementioned *Adam* magazine and the Hollywood-based Fax record label. The two partners released a series of risqué, sex-obsessed records that set an erotic monster in motion.

Stag records featured live "blue" comedy sets and "service songs" that told tales of action abroad – not all of it military! Presumably appealing to an audience with experience of the war, service songs became the cheap and cheerful staple of the stag party record.

The *Adam* party record came in two versions, one with respectable covers to be sold in the local store and a mail-order version that featured full-frontal nudes. The latter would arrive with stickers concealing the model's prize assets. As the mailman's steps could be heard fading from the front path, so the elaborate and undoubtedly edifying process of removing this last bastion of decency would begin. The surreptitious pleasure in revealing all must have been immense. All that there remained to do was the little matter of listening to the record and tucking the sleeve away with its vinyl brothers and sisters.

Like baseball cards for adults, stag party records could be collected. Perused at leisure, the set was an encyclopedia of erotica for the record-buying voyeur.

HOLLYWOOD'S MOST INTIMATE
SMOKER STORIES ⫶ BY MR. X ⫶

FAX 1015N

FAX RECORDS

THIS IS A REMOVABLE LABEL

You can remove this label easily without damaging the photo underneath. Start at corner and peel carefully.

The Record Labels

As naked vinyl flourished, so the record labels on the East and West coasts of America used it as an excuse to release as much crass comedy and trashy songs as they could record. In the process, the companies vied to produce outlandish record covers and succeeded in releasing some of the funniest and most offensive records imaginable.

Fax was the most prolific exponent of naked vinyl. It was based in LA and had a "stag party" series, a "personality" series, a special "erotica" series, and a "themes and scenes motion picture set" series. With Hollywood so close, the "themes and scenes" series was an almost inevitable addition to Fax's roster and it provided a backyard montage of life in Hollywood. The series featured aspiring actresses and actors acting out plays with a sexual theme – often bedroom farce based around the male quest for sexual fulfilment.

The "erotica" series featured some amazing records that were in keeping with the vinyl trend for documentary records, from the serious to the sociological and sublime. These were records about sex in all its forms; sex as both education and entertainment. Sociological and fictional erotica abounded; erotic plays, biographies, dialogue, and sexual exposés all tapped an overheated market.

The public lapped them up and hundreds were released, no matter how obscure and unusual; many a youth's sex education began with a sneaky glance at the parental record collection.

Laff focused its output around the American nightclub comedy circuit, also based in LA. It released records by "a parade of clowns and jesters" using the same winning formula of nightclub comedy and nude covers. As the records themselves tell us: "Recorded at the scene of the applause, on the stage, or at the intimate party, the live and living heart-tugging, button-busting laughter of America's funniest comic personalities, on Laff records just for you!!! Have a party, have a LAFF."

Fax and Laff were intertwined with Hollywood and many of their releases reflected this, inviting the listener into an intimate world populated by the rich, famous, and sexually successful. The records offered a personal invite to an exclusive soirée: "In every other respect you are there, an insider, rubbing shoulders with Hollywood greats at an intimate party." In an era obsessed with celebrity and stardom, this was an alluring idea and the records let the listener join an elite club, albeit only temporarily.

On the East Coast it was saucy song that was more in vogue and New York labels Davis and Que toyed with the traditions of Vaudeville for their erotic output. Davis Records, run by Joe Davis, had a roster of stars that churned out the *double entendre* songs that had been popularized on stage. Dubbed "special material", they were songs about sex that were hidden behind an altogether different theme and Joe Davis both presented and wrote many of the songs and ran the label. Davis and its sister label Beacon – whose catch line was "it's always 'party time' with 'Davis' LP albums" – gave the genre what it really deserved: talented entertainers and a classic line in naked covers.

Que had a similar output, along with records that were dubbed "sexucational" – songs and tales to inform the uninitiated in the art of all things carnal.

The Fax and Davis records in particular were wonderfully made and featured some outlandish titles – *My Pussy Belongs To Daddy* – and spectacularly rude covers. Not afraid to wade into a minefield of dubious morality, they complemented this bravado with some beautiful, shiny, deliciously nude covers and production values that were second to none.

It was an exciting time and vinyl was an exciting and intimate medium. Era and album came together beautifully to sell sex and comedy to the willing citizens of post-war America. The original labels are now defunct but the records remain as testimony to a time of blatantly sexist largesse.

Comedy and Culture

The comedians featured in this book were not superstars. While they may have played in the same nightclubs as those who were, it was most definitely on different nights. These people all had charm, wit, and a battery of jokes, some of which were truly awful.

The male comedians had charisma in abundance and sex on the brain. Bert Henry, Stu Gilliam, Rex Benson, and others had their repertoires recorded and their style can be catalogued in unison – filed under "blue" and saved for posterity. Their jokes could be funny and forgettable, offensive and off-the-wall; while the targets of their comedy were traditional ones: wives, mothers-in-law, sex, and alcohol. They were rapid fire, coarse, and crude, and while the laughter on record is at times a little thin, more often than not it's genuine and hearty.

Their female compatriots were entertainers more than comedians. Theirs was a sultry performance combined with cautionary tales to the young and innocent – "keep your knees together daughter!" Entertainers from the Vaudeville tradition, their shows were multi-faceted, frivolous, and fun.

Faye Richmond, Madame Mame, Terri "Cupcake" O'Mason and others were all successful with this brand of comedy and song, and they toured the nightclubs of America feeding the sexual imaginations of a generation of nightclub patrons.

Women sang, the men told jokes, and the audience drank and laughed, while routines were woven around sexual feelings, frustrations, and adventures. The cosmopolitan, metropolitan in-crowd was duly entertained and the wild, wily comics had their day in the limelight.

Eventually, though, the world moved on, and as the era of stag-party culture faded, so a new era in the history of naked vinyl emerged.

Some of the comedians survived this cultural seachange, while others faded into comic obscurity. Stu Gilliam achieved the most success in his post stand-up career, becoming a successful TV actor. He starred in

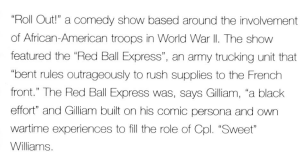

"Roll Out!" a comedy show based around the involvement of African-American troops in World War II. The show featured the "Red Ball Express", an army trucking unit that "bent rules outrageously to rush supplies to the French front." The Red Ball Express was, says Gilliam, "a black effort" and Gilliam built on his comic persona and own wartime experiences to fill the role of Cpl. "Sweet" Williams.

Gilliam also found himself on the frontline in real life, as there was "no place for a black as an entertainer in the Special Services". Instead he joined the infantry as "the Infantry had desegregation, they let you get shot together". His career continued in "Harris and Company" a "black-life series" that presaged *The Cosby Show* and battled against "the limited amounts of reasonable exposure" that African-American shows of the day received.

Beyond comedy and the stag-party scene, naked vinyl brought together hippy, swinger and rock culture to create covers themed around hard-won sexual liberation. Jimi

Hendrix's *Electric Ladyland*, epitomised this sub-genre and a host of rock-based copycat efforts followed. At the time the album came out, Jimi clearly had his doubts about the culture within which he was immersed – "the scene puts you through a lot of changes" he told journalist John Lombardi. While he had just cut his hair as "there are too many long-haired people running around whose heads aren't anywhere". As for the famous cover itself, he had nothing but contempt: "I didn't have nothing to do with that stupid LP cover they released".

In the latter half of the '60s, the fad for exotica continued unabated, and record labels scrambled to release music from the four corners of the world, seeking out cultural diversity with missionary-like zeal.

Finally, as the decade drew to a close, the bunny girl and buxom blonde were replaced by sunshine, love, and a pared down epitome of female beauty. Slender, beautiful, and bronzed, she was sexy and European and she was set to bring a touch of the catwalk to the album cover.

Into the '70s

Reinvented recently in finest post-modern fashion as a culturally rich melting pot of style, glamour, and fashion, in reality the '70s was far removed from this oasis of refinement. Most of the decade was spent fending off boredom with the many gimmicks that appeared. From The Bay City Rollers to The Village People, image and marketability won out over substance.

It was in this decade that naked vinyl became a tool to sell some of the most artistically-challenged music man has ever had the misfortune to create. Quite how a lot of it came to be released is a mystery, but more likely than not the music was a good excuse for a sexy cover because the two very rarely complemented one another. Take the fantastic Stef Meeder records featured later – amazing covers front the most innocuous middle-of-the-road cover versions played on the Hammond organ. There is nothing sexy about the music; as an aphrodisiac it is about as stimulating as wichedy grub soup. Yet it remains as evidence of the power of sex to sell.

Naked vinyl in the '70s was a heady mixture of enlightened European togetherness and American easy-listening schmaltz. Records appeared from Italy, England, Germany, France, and beyond; the albums formed a musical common market, featuring cover models from around the world. At once cosmopolitan and suburban, these were records for the "happy shopper" – cut-price, pretty, fun, and unspectacular music was packaged in a spectacular burst of colour, nudity, and design. $\rightarrow$

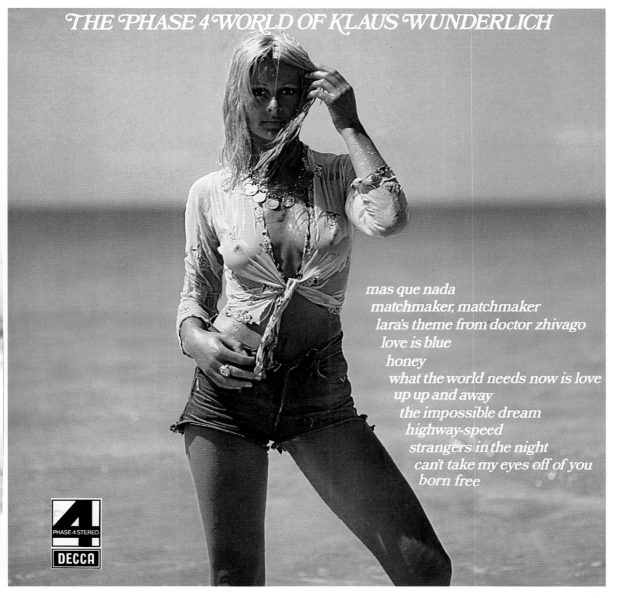

THE PHASE 4 WORLD OF KLAUS WUNDERLICH

mas que nada
matchmaker, matchmaker
lara's theme from doctor zhivago
love is blue
honey
what the world needs now is love
up up and away
the impossible dream
highway-speed
strangers in the night
can't take my eyes off of you
born free

PHASE 4 STEREO

DECCA

Easy-Listening

Musically, the '70s were a mixed bag; reggae, soul, funk, and rock may have been cool but the real and unassuming musical phenomena of the day was modern, upbeat easy-listening. We're not saying it was good, but it sure was successful.

"Airport music" was suddenly a valid form of musical expression and artist upon artist churned out all manner of insipid interpretations of the classic songs of the day. There were pop cover versions to remind you of your favourite stars, orchestral covers with a modern lilt, or covers of European classics designed to remind you of your package holiday and good times abroad. It was a winning formula, records sold, and session musicians the world over could sleep easy at night.

During the '70s, easy-listening was in love with cheesy cover versions, with cheesy covers, and the easy-listening phenomenon embraced naked vinyl with open arms. In return naked vinyl gave enhanced libido to unassuming

musical styles that, in reality, were long past their sell-by date. Nude covers were of use in adding a touch of glamour, sex, and mystery where none existed, and easy listening held on for dear life to the sexy image that naked vinyl provided.

The '70s easy-listening that is featured in this book falls into four categories: the Hammond medley; the smooth, sax-led cover version; "strings a go-go", screeching through countless popular classics; and the exotic extravaganza.

Continental exponents of the art of easy-listening created the devil's bistro that is the Hammond medley and no stone was left unturned to find the most unsuitable song for an organ makeover. Songs were mixed in insane combinations to produce three-minute classics of pop drivel. A minute each was all most of us could bear and, with a little drum solo to mark the change, our attention would be temporarily diverted from the music. Thereby distracted, we began our communion with the next slice of musical larceny. It was

the record labels that created this bizarre genre, forcing their Hammond stars to record popular classics much against their artistic will. In return we were given the nude cover as solace.

The saxophone was the preserve of Fausto Papetti and Gil Ventura, and they made it their own with all manner of smoochy cover versions. Gil Ventura even perfected the disco sax medley, though his version was more a sprint relay as he attempted to fit as many musical snippets as he could into each track. A sax rendition of "Light My Fire" overlapped the backing singers' vocal interpretation of "You Are the Sunshine of My Life", shortly to be followed by "Tomorrow", "Zodiac", and the "Theme From *Star Wars*".

The violin was as commonplace in the '70s as the sitar was in the late '60s, screeching its way through film scores, pop hits, and, of course, classical compositions. Orchestras such as the 101 Strings and the Silver Strings churned out album after album, and for some over- →

enthusiastic listeners, their ears will still be recovering.

The exotic extravaganza was a traditional tune that was played with a Western twang. Soon, modern, upbeat versions of what were once beautiful, traditional songs merged with takes on "La Viva España" or any half-decent European tune that fitted the bill. Albums would be themed around whichever country was fashionable that particular month – Hawaii or Togo – and the covers would follow suit, with a stereotypical image of naked native women coming up time after time, from continent to continent, in all manner of exotic-erotic poses. Hardly a culture escaped unscathed; from Borneo to the coasts of South America, native peoples could be forgiven for wanting to flee from these musical modernists for fear of the sound of bland, easy-listening cover versions being left ringing in their ears.

A lot of the albums made a play of the boom in overseas travel, and whereas '60s exotica had been about the music of mysterious countries that few had visited or would dare to try, '70s exotica was less far flung; its albums were themed around nearby countries that were visited during summer vacations abroad. It was about the package tour and a musical escape from the mundane, a reminder of the good times we've just enjoyed. Instant nostalgia and happy memories given a soundtrack.

To be fair, some good easy-listening music was made in this era. Klaus Wünderlich had a super-funky drummer to spice up his early efforts, and a nice turn in funky Hammond action, while Fausto Papetti produced the occasional spectacular drum breakdown amid a sea of sax. Robert Delgado was the king of the vacation album, with a nice turn in "latin lounge" and excellent upbeat covers of standards favoured by the hippies, such as "Be-In (Hare Krishna)".

Music though, who needs it? Well, I guess it's nice to have the whole package, but with the covers on offer, surely a little artistic meandering can be forgiven. The best '70s covers are blatant and up front, unashamed sleaze.

Gil Ventura toyed with sado-masochistic imagery, but his photos were delicate and orgasmic. Fausto Papetti used as many nudes as possible, seeming never to tire of what must have been a winning combination: middle-of-the-road sax covers and middle-of-the-night nude album covers. Meanwhile, Stef Meeder and Jaap Zeeland used the same photo shoot a dozen times – and if they hadn't been legally barred from releasing any more Hammond medleys, this series could have gone on forever.

The '70s continued in this happy vein, with musicians turning out anodyne, easy-listening for the tone-deaf masses. Looking back, the cover images remain fresh, with their pictorial style and period trimmings having matured well. As for '70s easy-listening...well, it's an acquired taste.

The '70s and Beyond

Disco went hand in hand with '70s easy-listening in its love for naked vinyl. It took it to its hedonistic heart and teased it in new directions, while in return naked vinyl offered the obvious expression for disco's heady outpouring of glitz, glamour, and sex.

Covers are adorned with the fashion accessories of the era – sequins, rollerskates, and Afro hair-dos – to reflect a lifestyle born of the party. Revelling in its own cocky self-belief and pleasure-seeking spirit, disco was about good times, and sex and music fitted the bill.

Throughout the course of the '70s, funk and disco toyed with naked vinyl and the most well-known efforts were those of The Ohio Players – a series of classic, so-near-yet-so-far nude covers that never quite revealed everything – and the sexy stylings of the Salsoul label. The mantle was firmly grasped by disco divas Silver Convention, and while their music was inferior, the faux disco "Get Up and Boogie" being their biggest hit, their covers captured disco times in a knowingly sexy way.

Disco was about the nightclub and that was about music, dancing, and sex; disco balls sparkled and lights spun, and the album art of '70s disco captured this world perfectly.

As the '70s drew to a close and society curled up into a conservative slumber, nudity was pushed out of the mainstream. Covers returned to safe and staid images. Sex was once again left to the imagination and naked vinyl all but came to an end to be replaced by the comic book nudity of heavy metal and the soft, nude chic of the erotic wall poster. In time, the compact disc came along and suddenly cover art was not such an issue. In a pared-down era who needed nudity, colour, and fun? Well, all of us of course, and eventually naked vinyl returned to centre stage, reinvented in a naughty '90s revival that embraced the imagery of the '60s and combined it with the sexy glamour of its own decade.

Music and style were plundered and designers were once again unafraid to use the naked body. And from lounge-core compilations and European easy-listening chic to the ultra-hip soulful house of New York's Naked Music, the summits of nudity are once again ready to be climbed.

Thanks for listening and we hope that you enjoy the book.

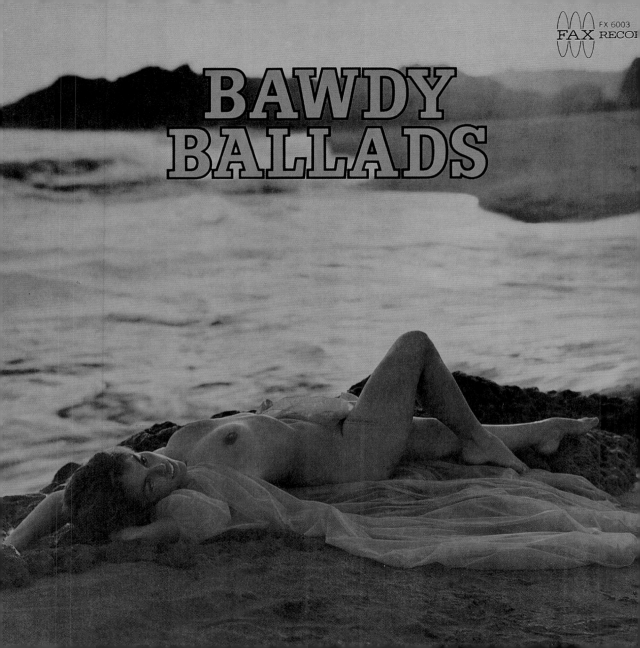

BAWDY BALLADS

FAX RECOI

FX 6003

1

The '50s:
Innocence Lost,
Paradise Found

Young Man and A Maid

"They were both naked, the man and his wife and they
were not ashamed."
Genesis Ch. 2 v. 25

**There could not be a more appropriate location to begin
our story than in the garden of Eden, the primordial
paradise where a naked Adam and Eve, the first
loving couple, grappled with temptation.** Did Eve get
to taste the succulent fruit she coveted? Of course she did,
because, thankfully for us, it was her disobedient act that
sowed the seeds which resulted in the rich bounty of
naked vinyl that is now laid before you.

Love is what the cover of *Young Man and A Maid* alludes
to, an album that provides a snapshot of folk song from
around the world – what it calls the "Love Songs of Many
Lands". These songs are of love found and virtue lost;

innocence replaced by experience and new life begun. The
titles "Where Does It Lead" and "Well Met, Pretty Maid" tell
of old-fashioned trials and tribulations, yet the basic themes
are relevant for all time. The sleeve notes by Nina Merrick
wax lyrical about the poetry of love and of the power exerted
by that most enigmatic of emotions:

"Of all we know, we know the most and the least about
love. It was born with the first man and maid, and has
continued to enchant and mystify us. It is untaught,
ambiguous, elusive, and overwhelming. Its time is every
season, and yet it can last a minute or an eternity. Love
is as different as those who house it."

And who could possibly argue with that?

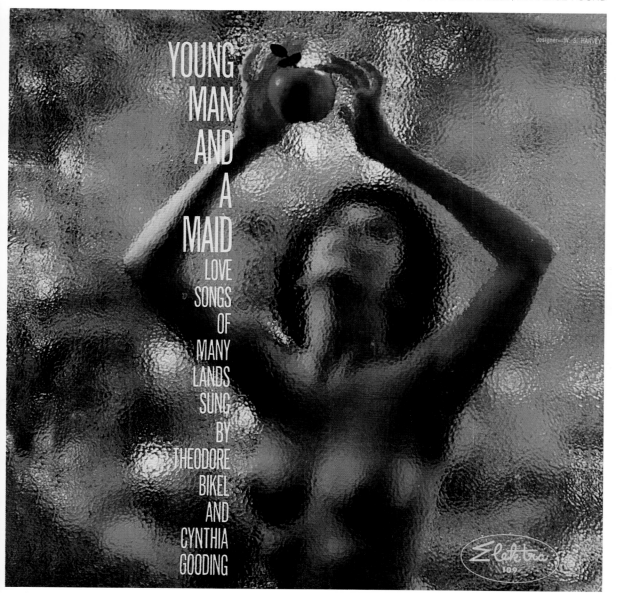

designer—W. S. HARVEY

YOUNG
MAN
AND
A
MAID
LOVE
SONGS
OF
MANY
LANDS
SUNG
BY
THEODORE
BIKEL
AND
CYNTHIA
GOODING

Elektra
109

String Jazz Quartet

Our classic selection from the '50s changes tempo from folk to jazz and the variety of pleasures to be gleaned from jazz's expression, artistry, and improvisation – all attributes held in abundance by the string quartet to be heard on this Vinnie Burke album, a foursome of whom Tom Stewart declares "not since the Gerry Mulligan Quartet…has a jazz group offered such a new and distinctive kind of sound as the String Jazz Quartet."

The album opens with the Dizzy Gillespie classic "A Night in Tunisia", but Vinnie's version offers a fresh take by reinterpreting the interludes between the solos, fulfilling the record's stated promise of a "Search for a New Sound". The refinement and innovation of Vinnie's departure from the musical norm is well matched by the marketing man's guile in dreaming up a winning formula for freedom of expression on a jazz album cover. "Sweet and Lovely" is one of the tracks on Side Two, but it could just as easily be a description of the curvaceous mover pictured naked on the front sleeve in an echo of the opening credits to a James Bond film. The name's Burke…Vinnie Burke, stirred but not shaken and licensed to play jazz.

Vinnie Burke's

STRING JAZZ QUARTET

ABC-PARAMO
FULL COLOR FIDE
ABC 170

FRAN SCOTT

Passion!

We move now from artistic expression in jazz to the rich Latin lexicon of love, embodied by the "Tangos and Torrid Tempos" of Walter Scharf's *Passion!*

Walter brings his Hollywood background to bear with an epic orchestral Latin "score" that is "sensitive and sensual". His music "does things to you", we are told, and after "the flames of the tangos warm your heart", the album "bursts brightly" into the excitement of sambas and rhumbas.

The cover itself is a seductive portrait (note the yellow rose on the window sill) that manages to convey a combination of romance and desire entirely appropriate to an album with songs as musically fevered and fervent as "Congo Flute" and "Love with Maracas". The copious sleeve notes espouse the virtues of the sensual and hot-blooded Latin and his tempestuous love-making with a literary flair unmatched since the ink in Casanova's feather quill ran dry.

With *Passion!* we are a step closer to the carnal.

jubilee **LP** HI FI

1079

jubilee **S** STEREO SONIC

WARNING!
USE ONLY WITH STEREO CARTRIDGE, OTHERWISE
SERIOUS DAMAGE MAY OCCUR IF USED WITH
MONAURAL PICKUP.

PASSION! *
walter scharf & his orchestra

Hawaii

People in the '50s may have been busy with love and romance, but there was still time left for other interests. Foremost among these, at least as far as the record industry was concerned, were travel and the exotic. Such popular themes of the era deserved some first-class nude album cover art, and Audio Fidelity proved more than capable of providing it for the packaging of the company's "studies in stereophonic HIGH FIDELITY sound". Sold on the excellent quality of their sound reproduction, these albums brought to the purchasers' living rooms the music of the world while at the same time conveniently seeking to showcase the attractive women that inhabited these seemingly faraway lands.

In this vein, Johnny Pineapple, a native of Honolulu who was acclaimed as "the foremost living interpreter of South Pacific music", served up music in an authentic Hawaiian manner, inspired by the scantily clad, luscious-looking lady with a flowing, flower-adorned mane. "Delightful and mellifluous" chime the sleeve notes, informing us about Hawaiian musical traditions and the islanders' fondness for reinterpreting North and South American tunes in their own distinct way, with "lilting rhythms and unique lyrical melodic style".

By simply slipping the record on to your stereo, turning the heating up full blast, swaying a little, and squinting at the cover, you could almost make yourself believe you were in Hawaii. Better still, take a vacation and see the real thing – you might get to find out what's behind those palm leaves.

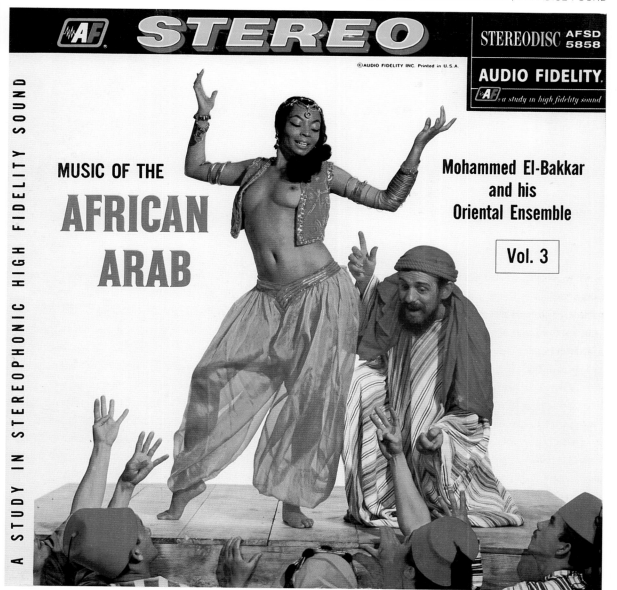

A Little Spice

From the innocence of our first piece of cover art set in the garden of Eden, we now enter an era when record labels and album cover art began to dispense with subtlety and allusion in favour of something just that little bit more overtly saucy. It was the record labels of New York City and Los Angeles that set about lowering the vinyl tone, and in no time at all, nudity had broken forth and nipples had been liberated, much to the delight of the average male record buyer.

At first glance, the cover of *A little Spice* appears to be a simple and sexy affair, but look more closely and its more surreal qualities come to the fore. Our sex kitten is in fact a floating torso and the cut-and-paste montage of the cover has a touch of the Salvador Dalí–Luis Buñuel about it. Davis Records should have included a song to match the image –

"When you kiss me, Gala, my moustache turns up too" would have added a little Spanish vigour to the proceedings.

Faye Richmonde spreads the gospel of sauciness in a compellingly seductive manner, opening with the classic "If I Can't Sell It, I'll Keep Sittin' On It". What may seem to be a song about a chair sale at a second-hand furniture store, might just have a deeper meaning lurking somewhere below the surface: "Look at that tempting body, it's so shapely to the eyes / and it will stand up under any weight or size."

The album's sleeve notes provide a little insight into the heritage of the songs, telling us that: "When night clubs and Vaudeville flourished, songs of this nature that had 'a little spice' were show stoppers." And if the eye-catching cover girl were to invite you to "Come Up And See Me, Anytime", it might have some effect on your bodily momentum too.

A little Spice

sung by FAYE RICHMONDE

IF I CAN'T SELL IT I'LL KEEP SITTIN' ON IT
THE DENTIST SONG
NAGGIN' WILL NOT HOLD A MAN
SHE'S NINE MONTH'S GONE FROM HOME
HANDY ANDY
I WANT A MAN TO GIMME SOME LUCK
COME UP AND SEE ME, ANYTIME
FIND OUT WHAT THEY LIKE
EP YOUR NOSE OUT OF MAMA'S BUSINESS
IF YOU CAN'T GET FIVE, TAKE TWO
NEVER BRAG ABOUT YOUR MAN
MAN O' WAR

Sing a Song of Sex:
The Double Entendre Holds Its Own

The sexual *double entendre* song had been a feature of the American entertainment industry for a long time before it found expression in LP form, when it was also given a little extra shelf life courtesy of a few record labels who provided the music with the covers it deserved. Joe Davis both wrote these types of songs for his albums and owned the record labels through which they were released, and it is from this insider's vantage point that he tells us something of the history of such compositions: "For the past 25 years, artists of renown such as Ethel Waters, Sophie Tucker, Pearl Bailey, and the late Bessie Smith made their mark in the entertainment world by singing songs known in the music business as 'special material'." This 'special material'

consisted of songs that were themed around one thing but sung to be very much about another. They were a clever way to break sexual taboos on stage and they brought the house down."

The singers featured in *Naked Vinyl* were not in the league of the aforementioned artists, but they did sing popular songs of the day in a sensual and entertaining fashion. The songs themselves leave little to the imagination and here are the titles, some with a lyric, that best capture a genre that proved so popular:

"Come Up and See Me, Anytime" –
"When it comes to baking pies, I'm the best /
so when you feel like pastry, won't you be my guest."

"Now feel that nice soft bottom built for wear or tear, I really hate to part with such a lovely chair." Faye Richmonde

"Handy Andy" –
"Although he looks as small as Gandhi,
in Spain they call him Mucho-Grande, /
oh how his muscles can expandy, Handy Andy of mine."

"I Never Saw Such Knockers" –
"I never saw such knockers before, /
like those knockers on my girlfriend's front door /
I like to feast my eyes on knockers this size, /
'cause to me they'll certainly win any prize."

"How Far Should A Good Girl Go?"
"I'm Wild About That Thing"
"In The Shade of Her Apple Tree"
"I Blew Louie in St Louie"
"I'm A Virgin But I'm on the Verge"
"All The Girls Like Big Dick"
"It Was Hard When I Kissed Her Goodbye"
"Quit Your Feelin' Around"
"How Do Worms Make Love?"
"Get Your Mind Out of the Gutter!"

Sexarama

Sexarama indeed, and along with the sledgehammer-subtlety of the title we are served up a heady cocktail of smut and song – in short, another Davis Records' classic in the making. The charms of the sultry señorita are clear for all to see, although the judicious use of Gypsy lace helps to preserve a little modesty, and we are left in no doubt that, as Miss Dee sings:

"They say it pays to advertise, so I'm here to announce, it's what's up front that counts. / When you need some loving and your long day is done, it's what's up front that counts. / While you're young and healthy, live it up and play, it's what's up front that counts."

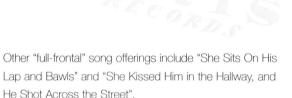

Other "full-frontal" song offerings include "She Sits On His Lap and Bawls" and "She Kissed Him in the Hallway, and He Shot Across the Street".

Davis Records didn't rely solely on nude covers and sexy songs for its output, also releasing such fine fare as the delicious *Pizza Party* and the romantic *To My Wife*. In the same series, any doubts about the morality of the whole enterprise might have been assuaged by the inclusion of *Hymns of Faith*.

FOR ADULTS ONLY

JD-120

AVIS
RECORDS
High Fidelity Recording

SEXARAMA

Sung by MISS DEE

IT'S WHAT'S UP FRONT THAT COUNTS
HOW FAR SHOULD A GOOD GIRL GO?
I'M WILD ABOUT THAT THING
FOR MEN ONLY
SHE SITS ON HIS LAP AND BAWLS
MRS. KANNER'S CAN
THINGS ARE SOFT FOR GRANDMA
SHE KISSED HIM IN THE HALLWAY,
    AND HE SHOT ACROSS THE STREET
HEY, MISTER ICEMAN
OH WHAT A JOCK
HE BROKE IT OFF INSIDE OF HER
SWEET FAT MAMA

For Women Only

Apparently, the marketing department at Davis Records was determined to appeal to a female market as well as to the males of the species, and although we have our suspicions about who this record was truly aimed at, *For Women Only* at least purports to offer women their very own record of saucy songs.

In fact, this is a unique album cover, in that it's the only male "nude" that we could find. (Sorry about that girls, but the chances of actually seeing a pecker on one of these covers is less than zero.) But by including *For Women Only*, at least we've attempted to counter the rampant sexism that inspired the cover art collected here in *Naked Vinyl*.

But was this record really "For Women Only" back then – surely they were too busy baking apple pie? How many women would have bought this record? Would women, for example, have been interested in "He's the Queen of Fire Island"? We have to say that we have our doubts. We suspect that Davis Records was making an early play for the gay market – too early, since the market didn't yet exist in the '50s! (It was also too early for digital retouching technology – note the grass still attached to our hero's feet.)

The songs are all sung by one Saul T. Peter, a pseudonym with a euphemistic lilt if you pronounce it as intended – Peter being slang for the male member, in case you weren't sure.

Hot Pepper

With this next serving of vinyl spice, our young Morticia look-alike so nearly reveals all, but instead, alas, her dignity is saved by a well-positioned nightie. With its snappy design, tangy colours, and looks that fan the flames of desire (and scare us half to death at the same time), we feel *Hot Pepper* stakes a sure claim to a place in the marble halls of all-time vinyl nudity.

The record presents an all-star cast, including the fair Faye Richmonde, Miss Dee, and the unforgettable (and recently mentioned) Saul T. Peter. Among the extraordinarily direct *double entendre* songs on this album are "You Ought To See Her Box" and "Tony's Got Hot Nuts" – the all-star cast must have relished the opportunity to wrap their vocal cords around the lyrics of the classic number "She Likes to Lick, Lick, Lick":

"She used to lick, lick, lick on her liquorice stick, when she was very young / and an ice-cream cup, she could lap it up, she knew how to use her tongue. / Now she's much older and much bolder, she's just turned seventeen / and she still lick, lick, licks on her liquorice stick if you know what I mean."

Pages 57–58: A platter of pussy in the form of the albums *My Pussy Belongs to Daddy*, complete with the strategically placed feline star itself, and *Pussy Galore*. If this were the real Miss Moneypenny, would such an open relationship have stood the test of time? Perhaps James Bond was right to stick with the devil he knew, although with an early morning wake-up call like this on offer, the temptation must have been hard to resist – 007 might be forgiven for saying, "Can I put you on hold, something's just popped up".

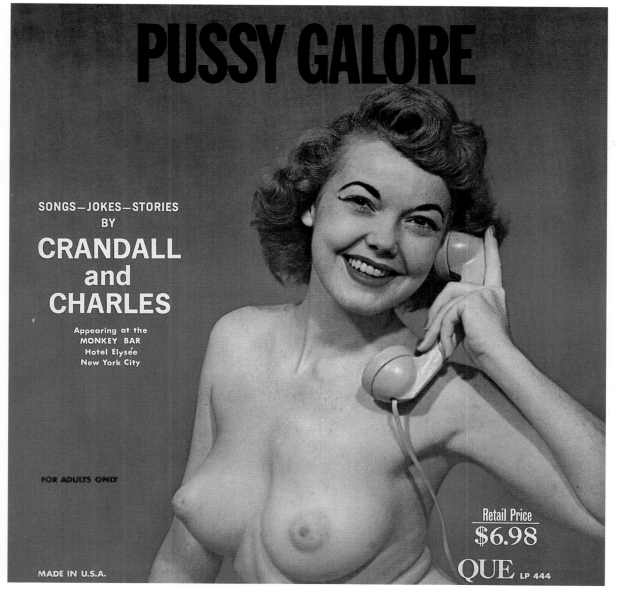

Instant Sex

On this classic album "for mature people", Madame Mame serves up a selection of "sexucational" songs that leave little to the imagination, and these tunes come to us courtesy of Que, a New York record label of impeccable credentials.

In her theme song, "Instant Sex", Madame Mame philosophizes about the '50s craze for "instant" products. Is this good or bad, she muses, before deciding that, when it comes to sex, instant is where it's at – although it is unclear whether she intended instant to mean "quick" as well as "now". We would guess the latter.

"'We're living in instant times," Madame Mame sings and sex is no exception: "Instant this and instant that, is all you hear today, / is that bad or is that good, here's all I have to say. / You've got to have instant sex or you're not with it, / instant sex, you'd better believe it, / it's so easy to define, we're living in instant times. / You've gotta have instant sex or you're a loser, instant sex a super infuser, / you can get it for a dime, we're living in instant times."

In the same mould, the cover is either a Warholesque depiction of one side of life in '50s America or it is a nice picture of Madame Mame's chest – the choice is yours.

INSTANT SEX

STANT SEX
NEVER SAW SUCH KNOCKERS
'S A FAIRY NICE FELLOW
TER THE BALLS
TTER COME BILL BAILEY
THE SHADE OF HER APPLE TREE
LEW LOUIE IN ST. LOUIE
YOU THINK YOU GOT IT HARD
GOT A HANDFUL OF NUTS
THERMOMETER MAN
KE YOUR HAND OFF OF IT
WANNA DO IT RIGHT NOW
EP YOUR KNEES TOGETHER DAUGHTER

Sexucational Songs
sung by
MADAME MAME

QUE LP 445

MADE IN U.S.A.

Retail Price
$6.98

Adam Magazine

What is your sex IQ?

1. What is sex?
   a. A depressant
   b. A form of expression
   c. A state of mind

2. Do you think Al Fresco sex is harmful?
   a. Only when done outdoors
   b. If I did I wouldn't be planning a hike
   c. No, but the grass stains give you away

Adam magazine was an adventure mag from the '50s that reinvented itself as a sophisticated slice of soft-porn cheekiness. Its pages, which displayed an obsession with the female of the species, were filled with erotic stories, sex quizzes, and tips on dating and the art of love, along with articles about Hollywood, stripping, and anything remotely to do with sex. The Adam empire also published calendars, books, bedside readers, and, fortunately for us, also turned its hand to coronary-inducing risqué records.

Adam's sexual politics were clear: women knew perfectly well how to stick up for themselves and what men were going to try to do was break down their stout defences. The women who featured in the magazine were busty models and generally involved in some way in the entertainment industry, but they were natural and feminine and the magazine was exotically illustrated, well written, and entertaining.

A spoof quiz was among the many features that made the magazine what it was, together with the monthly advice column of Althea Currier who – single and 23, a burlesque star and actress who "checks out at 38–24–35 in the vital areas" – told it like it was. A male reader wrote: "My problem is that I don't know what to say to girls. Laugh if

!Adam!

you want but please tell me how you rate a man." Althea replied: "Well, I rate a man by the way he acts and treats me, and believe me I'm grateful for a gentleman." But when it comes to dating: "All I can say is that when a guy takes a girl out and shows her a good time on the town, the girl is going to feel pretty damn insulted if the guy doesn't at least try to kiss her goodnight." Her final words of wisdom: "Get out there and hustle, David. You'll find it's easier than you think!"

The small ads offered books for sale, such as *The Many Loves of Jacques Casanova* and *An Uncensored History of Pornography*, while other items included "strip checkers" and "the kind of exciting films you have been looking for!…new movies! Spanking, wrestling, bondage".

Among the above, and often featured in their own right, were the ads for the latest albums that *Adam* and its business partner, Fax Records, had recently released. The most popular of these was the *Adam* Stag Party

record series, whose style was simple – a topless model posed in a studio, with nothing more than the odd prop and a smile or pout for company, would front ribald record compilations of bawdy songs or comedy.

Adam magazine continued its characteristic output well into the '60s, and although it doesn't pretend to be an advert for equality, as a catalyst for the rise of the nude album cover, its contribution stands unequalled.

FAX
FX 60
REC

HOLLYWOOD'S MOST INTIMATE SMOKER STORIES
BY MR. X

2

The '60s:
Original Sin

Adam Stag Party Record 1

The *Adam* stag party record appeals directly to the record buyers of America with memories of World War II and the cultural changes that went with it. This market, brought up on "nude photos passed around the barracks", long had an eye for the female nude and they had the disposable income to make Adam's erotic investment a success. Each one of the *Adam* stag records was spectacular, with a feast of nakedness to accompany the gags, stories, and songs. We could have selected them all,

but due to limitations of space, it seemed best to choose a few of the company's finest offerings.

Unsurprisingly, *Adam Stag Party Record 1* was a big hit. The album was the first in a collaboration between *Adam* magazine, one of the leading men's magazines of the era, and Fax Records. For the men of the time, this partnership made for a winning combination of buxom model and cute comedy, setting the scene for a series that ran to 11 saucy selections.

Pages 68–69: *The Stag Party Special* was a record dedicated to the "bachelors and broad-minded men" of America and this '60s institution – a "sex-o-rama" of song and mirth – provided the best excuse possible to serve up the nudity we love to see.

FAXLP 1006
FAX RECORDS

Adam
STAG PARTY RECORD

1

STORIES
MOTHER «
NEVER «««
TOLD «««
FEATURING
BUZZY «
GREENE

ADAM STAG PARTY SPECIAL   FAXLP 1006

$5.98

FAX
RECORDS
FAXLP 1006
A HIGH FIDELITY RECORDING

Adam
PARTY RECORD

33⅓ RPM LONG PLAY RECORD ALBUM

STAG PARTY SPECIAL
VOLUME ONE

ADAM MAGAZINE presents th
wildest sexcapade of stag par
humor ever put on record!

featuring the fabulous BUZZY GREENE at his sizzling bes

FAX RECORDS
FAXLP 1006
A HIGH FIDELITY RECORDING

COPYRIGHT 1959, FAX RECORD COMPANY

MADE IN U.S.A.

PRINTED IN U.S.A.

A GENUINE
ADAM PARTY RECORD
BY THE EDITORS OF
ADAM MAGAZINE

STAG PARTY SPECIAL

VOLUME ONE

At Last, A Party Record Worthy Of Its Name!

Women blush, girls scream, men roar with delight and approval when they hear this thrilling sex-o-rama of stag party gags and stories by the fantastic Buzzy Greene. Every torrid bit of his explosive dialogue has been captured in this great recording; guaranteed to send any audience or party into convulsive fits of uncontrollable mirth. This is the first of a great new series of party records brought to you by the most exciting man's magazine in America . . . ADAM Magazine. Don't miss a single ADAM party record!

HERE IS THE ONE RECORD YOU MUST HAVE TO PUT LIFE INTO YOUR PARTY AND SPICE INTO YOUR LIFE!

SIDE ONE

• Up-John Cocktail • Piledriver • The Acrobat and Her Orange • Girls Who Wear Glasses • Long Arm Of The Law • The Gay Boys • Everything's Big In Texas • Undertaker's Delight • Riding The Bus • The Bashful Bride • The Egyptian Girl • Seventeen Daughters • Person To Person • Japanese Industrialist • The Bartender Story • Artificial Respiration • Her Pink Seat • The Sexy Office Girl • The Boss's Big Surprise.

SIDE TWO

• Teacher's Pet • Cute Little Girl • Men's Room Caper • The Glass Eye • The Ball Game • The Perfect Ass • Queen And The Bulls • The Pet Duck • A Man's Brassiere • Confucius Say Many Things • The Sexy Indian • Her Body Beautiful • Las Vegas Bust • Marriage Problems • Jock And Jean • Self Pleasure • Fur Coat Hoax • I Don't Know What's Got Into You • Secret Love • Mule Train • Bewitched, Bothered, And? • Dreams • On Top Of Some Oakie • Wild Goose • Standing In The Pool Room • Lola Wants • It's Magic.

BUZZY GREENE
MOTHBALL OF INSANITY

This is just one of the zany nicknames that has been hung on Buzz Greene, the West Coast's long established, most uproarious and naughty comedian.

Buzz is a comic's comic. That means he's one of the rare few who can roll his colleagues in the aisle without shutting off the paying customers from his intensely personal howlers.

There has to be a reason, and there is. Buzz is just about the only living American comedian who writes all his own stuff. No staff of gagmen cooks up his jokes—though plenty of them "borrow" from him for other comics. Says Buzz, "I got the habit of brewing my own buzziness when I was in burlesque and too broke to hire writers. The hell of it is, I haven't been able to break the habit since."

Outside of burlesque, in which he starred for almost 20 years, Buzz has toured the world many times for USO Shows, played saloons (one for 14 years!), been featured in scores of film and TV roles. When he isn't getting yuks solo, he doubles as a top character actor. Buzz is a real one-man gang.

So much so, in fact, that he can fix anything, from a fellow-comic's ailing gag to the plumbing backstage or the electrical wiring. "I belong to so many unions," he says, "that I have to keep working just to pay my dues."

Adam Stag Party Record 3, 8, and 9

Adam Stag Party Record 3 begged inclusion for a couple of very obvous reasons! The record features the "shocking humor" of the prolific comedian Bert Henry (see pages 76–77). "You'll die laughing" the back cover notes tell us – unless, that is, something else has you choking for air first…

The series continues with *Adam Stag Party Record 8,* a theatrical masterpiece that offers proof that blondes don't have all the fun. The model is the luscious Beverley Hills (her stage name, in case you weren't quite sure), who in 1961 was "the queen of Hollywood exotic dancing"; as to whether she still holds the crown, we're not too sure.

A Night of Bedlam features "the lusty folk songs and erotic ballads that have titillated fun-loving adults for generations".

Side One opens with "'Get Along Home Cindy", which contains the lusty lines: "She took me to her chamber. She throwed my clothes away." Side Two contains a memorable and tearful ballad about the trials and tribulations of a prostitute known as "Poor Lillian", who "With sailors…started losing face when she concealed her naval base".

On *Adam Stag Party Record 9* we're invited by the exotic-looking Tanya Murietta – "a fiery blend of lioness and lamb" – to "SIN along with us"; Tanya certainly knows how to get a deadly serpent moving. We're given more "wild party songs", featuring tales of "betrayed maidens, hard-drinking men, and lusty adventurers", which should just about cover the entire readership of this book.

FAXLP1012
FAX RECORDS

Adam
STAG
PARTY
RECORD
3
SHOCKING
HUMOR ‹‹‹
FEATURING
›› BERT ‹‹
HENRY

Adam Stag Party Record 10 and 11

These two records were compilations of "lusty service songs", offering a nostalgic collection that would not only remind old soldiers of the comradeship forged in the "Hell Holes of the world" but also convince them, by means of delicious nude album covers, that all the years of endured hardship had been worthwhile.

On *Adam Stag Party Record 10: Off Limits*, the cover girl settles down to strum her guitar, and we're offered an album full of "scorching ballads" that dwell on the finer points of off-shore leave and the nature of female generosity overseas in times of trouble, where "the women don't smell like roses, but they know 100 poses".

It's back to a bewitching blonde again on *Adam Stag Party Record 11: Further Off Limits*, and another helping of the songs that "provided a safety valve for men under stress". With tales of "hard-drinking men, jaded whores, and bad food" it's difficult to believe there was a war going on – or perhaps these were some of the stress-inducing unpleasantries a serviceman in the right theatre of action battled against…

More stylish pearls of poetic balladry are here, such as the classic "Take Her Down".

Wild service songs, we're told in the sleeve notes, are a "vital part of history and culture".

FAXLP 2002

FAX RECORDS

Adam
**STAG
PARTY
RECORD**
10
OFF«««
LIMITS«««
FEATURING
**WILD SERVICE
SONGS**«««

Songs for Adults Only

This album brings another stunning model and wig together with more "wild, funtastic, risqué" songs featuring the vocal talents of a brand new "sexation", Terri "Cup Cake" O'Mason, a sultry singer who is "hotter than a firecracker".

Terri wrote her own material and as the record begins she warns that "if you have your haloes on, you might want to take them off", before diving headlong into her theme song "Cup Cakes", whence her nickname came. Terri tells how she believed the way to a man's heart was through his stomach. But when she baked dinner for her boyfriend he didn't seem that impressed and her feelings were hurt – "until after dinner, I found out that (cue song) – 'he liked to nibble on my cupcakes. He just went nuts about their taste...'"

Later Terri relates the story of her stay in a house of ill-repute, though whether the story is factual or fictional we cannot say. Terri clearly enjoyed the experience and claims she was the best in her business until one day she made a discovery that changed everything. "I blew up in a terrible jit; 'cause when I found out the others got paid, I packed up my things and I quit".

The cause of her travails? Well it's either the booze –"oh baby, what that booze does to me" – or the men – "men are like socks, you gotta change 'em everyday". Either way Terri shoots straight form the hip and we like her style.

Bert Henry: A Man Obsessed

"What type of man is Bert Henry?" ask the sleeve notes to his top-selling album *Position Is Everything!!* On stage, "he can transform even the most sophisticated audience into a state of shrieking, blushing, gasping, helplessness", while offstage he is "quiet and mild mannered". The record may be overstating Bert's talents just a touch, but there is no doubt that he was a funny and endearing entertainer. Bert may appear to be a bar-room rogue (who, in his own words, is "about as sexy as an olive with its pimento hanging out"), but in reality he is a happily married family man, although as he said, "I can never divorce my wife because I can never find a girl that good looking with such bad eyesight."

One of the comic kings of "naked vinyl" and a star of the Fax comedy roster, Bert Henry's humour is punchy and "blue", the product of America's West Coast nightclub comedy circuit, with its wealthy audiences, loud laughter, and thick cigar smoke. Henry's routine was based around booze, broads, and sex, while his jokes were usually at the expense of his wife or mother-in-law. He had a self-deprecating style, a Phil Silver-esque delivery, and, like the naked vinyl that bore his name, subtlety was put to one side. Oh, and he had one more thing – some very bad jokes.

"My parents raised me to be a sex maniac, but I couldn't pass the physical."

"Confucius say 'man who makes love on ground has piece on earth'."

The titles of his live comedy albums, such as *The Hard Way*, *At the Hungry Thigh*, and *Position Is Everything!!*, leave little to the imagination, but they are evidence of his non-prudish style, while the jokes themselves prove that there's no accounting for taste.

"'A woman should always wait for the right man to come along, but it's a good idea to get married in the meantime."

THE UNCENSORED HUMOR OF BERT HENRY

A BLISTERING MADCAP OF SMOKER STORIES

FAX RECORDS

FAXLP 3001

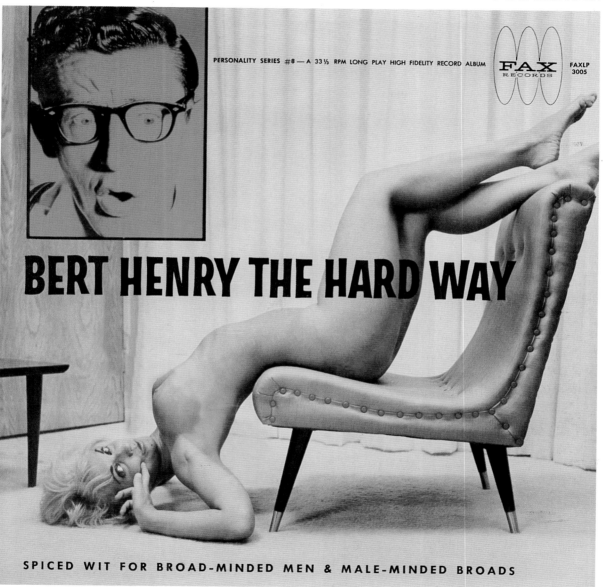

PERSONALITY SERIES #8 — A 33⅓ RPM LONG PLAY HIGH FIDELITY RECORD ALBUM

FAX RECORDS

FAXLP 3005

BERT HENRY THE HARD WAY

SPICED WIT FOR BROAD-MINDED MEN & MALE-MINDED BROADS

Giggles for Guzzlers

The liberal West Coast had been home to the movie industry for decades by the '60s. Later that decade there was "free love" in San Francisco, but Hollywood had had its own more dubious means of free love ever since the moguls, studios, and unprincipled hangers-on had developed the mass entertainment industry and begun its insatiable consumption of many a starstruck teenage girl's career dreams. Too numerous to all become movie stars, at least straight away, this willing cast of aspiring actresses, models, singers, and comedians all needed to find ways to earn a living in the meantime. And here record labels such as Fax helped to play a part: aural talent went out on the record, while visually attractive talent adorned the cover and sold it to the consumer. Everyone was happy and, from the would-be starlet's point of view, you never knew, if you were lucky you might just catch the eye of someone important.

The Bolo label was an offshoot of Fax and here they put out *Giggles for Guzzlers* by Beryl Williams "The Laugh A Minute Man". We think it's a drink in a club that you're meant to be guzzling, but the cover girl might be enough to give you a thirst for something else. Williams was a novelty act and a stand-up comic with a reputation for devastating ad-libbing – not a man to heckle.

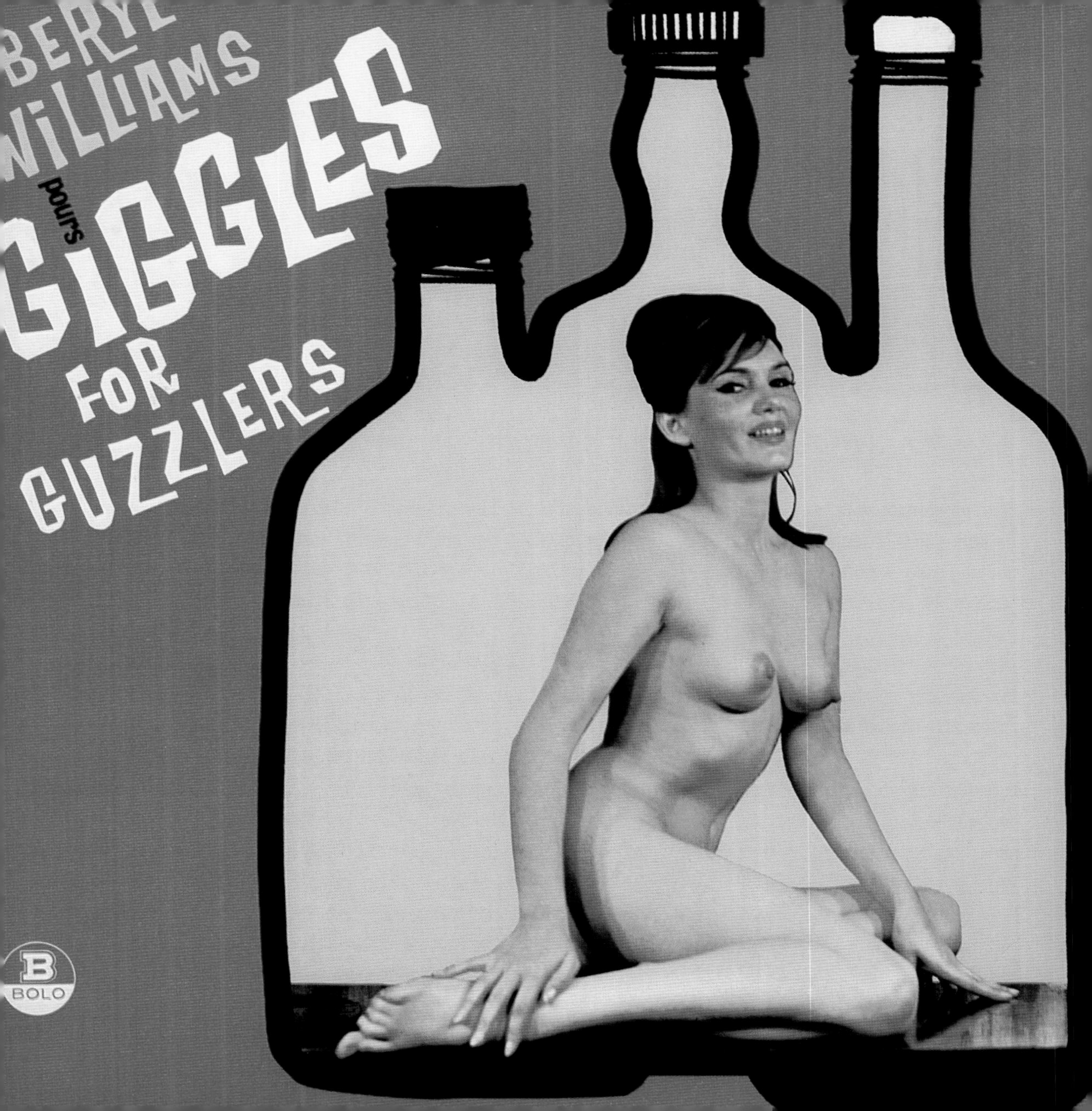
BERYL WILLIAMS
pours
GIGGLES
FOR
GUZZLERS
B
BOLO

Starlets and Strippers – Or How to Get Ahead in Hollywood Without Really Trying

The vinyl nude was born of many things, not least of which was the desire of young women to get ahead by any means possible. In the quest for success, record covers offered as good a place as any for girls to gain exposure, money, and experience. Many of the models featured in the pages of *Naked Vinyl* had been through Hollywood in one way or another – they were wanna-be starlets, dancers, strippers, and everyday girls moving up (or perhaps down) in the highly competitive world of entertainment. For example, the *Adam* stag series (see pages 66–73) included, among others, Jeanne Mack, a Hollywood starlet of "sultry temperament"; Beverley Hills; and Tanya Murietta.

June McCall, a successful actress herself, tells us that only a few actresses get "a firm toehold on the movies solely on the basis of their overpowering beauty or great dramatic talent". The majority had to fight for their day in the sun, and starlets and established actresses alike set out in a variety of imaginative and creative ways to try and generate positive publicity.

Tales abound of the stunts that they pulled in order to get noticed. Marie Wilson – a blonde who built a career out of being "darling but dumb" – came up with one attention-grabbing ploy: "Marie startled both pedestrians and motorists at the busy corner of Wilshire Boulevard and La Brea in Hollywood by chasing a chimpanzee up the street wearing only black panties and bra. When the scantily clad Marie finally pounced upon the chimp at the teeming intersection, spectators froze with mouths agape and two cars collided head on." Wilson got the news exposure she craved and extra work to go with it. Her stunt was pulled just outside the offices of Fax Records,

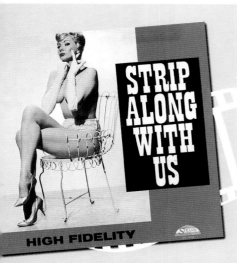

which was also based on La Brea Avenue in Los Angeles.

As an alternative career path, stripping was not without its merits. In America in the 1950s it was a big business. The York nightclub was one popular strip venue. It was run by owner Bill York, who "took over the joint upon his release from the Seabees". The eponymous club also featured comedy from Buzzy Greene, one of the comedy stars of naked vinyl. The customers got what they wanted – "good food, good drink, good music, and good looking gals removing their clothes to the beat, beat, beat of the tom-toms" – and the York became the "mother lode for the wildest strippers, comics, and spectators".

Many of the record labels that are featured in *Naked Vinyl* were based in Hollywood, and with all this talent on their doorstep, it's perhaps not surprising that their saucy output was so widespread and successful.

"...When the scantily clad Marie finally pounced upon the chimp at the teeming intersection, spectators froze with mouths agape and two cars collided head on."

Basin Street West

Stu Gilliam was a deadpan, slow-paced African-American comedian from Detroit who mumbled his way to merriment as he span "virgin yarns for the wicked" to raucous club crowds that appreciated "blue" humour. Other popular African-American comedians of the day, such as Redd Foxx and Rudy Ray Moore, were guaranteed sell-outs too. But in the segregation era Fax must have been tempted to play it safe; that they didn't suggests they knew who their audience was and they didn't feel it was controversial to opt for the sexy cover star.

As a boy Stu Gilliam was called upon to entertain at church and private functions, and you have to wonder what this same community would have made of his adult material.

Religious themes clearly influence some of his "scorching satire". Stu tells one tale of a New Orleans man meeting St Peter at the Pearly Gates:

" 'Why should I let you in?', St Peter asks. 'I'm cool baby. I'm an upstanding member of the community. I was even baptized in a white church in New Orleans.' St Peter is taken aback and questions his latest arrival about the events that occurred, eventually asking, 'The "minister" that baptized you, just how long did he hold your head under the water?' The main man thinks back, 'Well, we went down to the river and we were all dressed in white and the minister took hold of me and dunked me under and…damn, if that ain't the last thing I remember!'"

"stu gilliam"

at basin street west

FAX RECORDS

FAXLP-3006N

Seduction Bachelor Style

This is a Hollywood B-movie on vinyl – or, if the cover is anything to go by, is that Double D? It features Bryce Bond, "a truly talented actor, and a man of many facets" – and, of course, Bernadette, who plays, among others, an uneasily swayed "Beautiful Maid From Brooklyn".

The record is a bedroom farce based around the eternal male quest for sexual gratification – a "stalking male seeking to conquer the female". The story begins as our bachelor hero brings his quarry home: "OK doll, come on, right this way, this is my little kingdom you might say, away from everybody else", although things don't quite go all his own way – "Honey, that doesn't come off, that's my dress!" By the time we turn the record over and get to story number three, he and a lucky secretary from the 14th floor have a drive to Westchester planned, and as the record ends we're left to wonder if he has more success this time round.

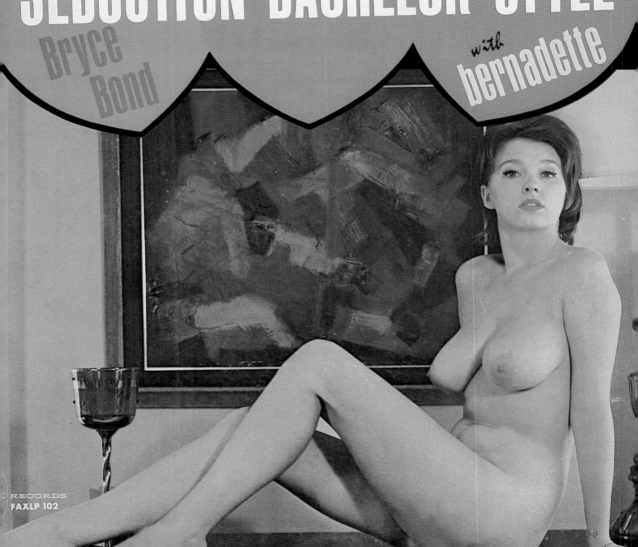

SEDUCTION BACHELOR STYLE

Bryce Bond

with **bernadette**

RECORDS
FAXLP 102

Sex is My Business

No need to guess what this record is all about – "sex" and "sin" are highlighted on the sleeve, and the hard reality of paid-for, loveless sex is what we get, from our call-girl cover star down to the very last groove.

Sex Is My Business is a real-life highlight from Fax's "Erotica" series, featuring stories from sex industry insiders – "actual interviews with prostitutes, homosexuals, pimps, and 'johns'". Billed as a documentary on record, this exposure of the seedier side of American life is compelling listening. And whereas most erotic records of the day dealt with the lighter side of sex, *Sex Is My Business* gets down to the really uncomfortable truth of the matter.

We listen to a call girl's lost innocence as she recalls her first experience of the trade: "I needed money to buy a ticket…she said 'I'll buy you your ticket'…she didn't mention what I had to do in return." More lurid and chilling still is her subsequent experience at a Hollywood party: "He was an actor, a big name, and I went to his house and I was shaking like a leaf because I loved him on the screen… guys started leaving and going to the bedrooms with girls, so he says to me 'you're gonna spend the night, so just relax and I'll tell the others to leave'…he takes me upstairs and he knows I'm scared and says 'go to bed' …I spent the night with him – we had sex two or three times that evening. I'd had sex before, but never with a man that old.'"

SEX IS MY BUSINESS

FAX RECORDS

FAXLP 1007

Sex On Record

Adults-only reading has been around for quite some time, but adults-only records seem like a novelty.
In fact, the sex record has been around for a long time and in many forms, from rehashing ancient erotica to trashy porn and the sounds of lovemaking. Fax Records had its own "erotica series", which contained such classic albums as *Nights of Love in Lesbos* – "a frankly intimate description of a sensuous young girl's lesbian desires" – and *Erotica: The Rhythms of Love*. These records were often not as rude as they sounded, but, of course, the covers made them something special.

But in the '60s sex on record even went hardcore, of sorts. Efforts such as *Humpingville USA* – "Smalltown Hicks Getting Their Kicks" – came with covers that were pure '60s' porn, with stories to match. Other favourites in this series included *Lustful Sexlife of a Perverted Nympho Housewife* – Russ Meyer would have been proud. For those seeking a change of cultural surroundings, even tourism was catered for with the release in 1970 of *Sex and Sin in Tijuana*. This companion to the sights and sounds of life in a border town in Mexico offered a "passport to the peoples and places of pleasure". Although more difficult to fold in half than a map, and difficult to refer to whenever you found yourself in a promising location, the record nevertheless detailed more interesting sights than the average tourist guide.

The movie soundtrack was another fertile genre. The most famous examples are the French erotic classics of the '70s, *Emmanuelle* and *Bilitis*. As films they were soft-focus, soft-porn that aimed to tell an erotic story in a stimulating way, while the soundtracks were dreamy orchestral epics that reflected the mood of the movies.

The vinyl revival has seen a host of sexy soundtracks reissued and back in vogue, including the groundbreaking *Deep Throat*, Russ Meyer's memorable efforts, and the horror film *Vampiros Lesbos,* directed by Franco Manera.

Long may it continue!

Emmanuelle

Fornicating Female Freaks –
"...actually hear them enjoying
'the forbidden' and frolicking
in orgiastic spasms of
sensuous delights"

Tales You'd Never Tell Mother

We come next to Laff Records, which, like Fax, was also based in Los Angeles. In the best traditions of America, Laff firmly believed that "big was beautiful". It featured more up-front comedy from the "showpeople dedicated to the humor of America". To you and me that would be comedians – those who "record their uproarious talents for your pleasure and unadulterated fun".

From a record entitled *Tales You'd Never Tell Mother*, I guess you'd expect to hear, well, some tales that you'd never tell your mother. Instead what we get is more "blue" comedy from Kenny Karol, with tales such as this: "This fellow didn't know what to get his wife for Christmas, so he bought her a live monkey. He took it home and his wife says, 'What's this?' And he says, 'It's your Christmas present'. So she says, 'Are you crazy? What's it gonna eat?' And he says 'Whatever we eat, the monkey'll eat.' She says, 'Where's the monkey gonna sleep?' And he says, 'We sleep in bed, the monkey'll sleep in bed with us.' So, finally, she says, 'What about the smell?' And he replies, 'I got used to it, the monkey'll get used to it too!'"

KENNY KAROL

TALES YOU'D
NEVER
TELL MOTHER

TWO LADIES OF THE EVENING
THE ICE MAN
INDIAN MAID
BELVIDENE HOTEL

LAFF
RECORDS

A5014

Courtin' on a Mule

We look up at her, she looks down at us and it's love at first sight. No doubt somewhere in America there is a statue dedicated to such a goddess. Perhaps the cover puts it best – "roasted to perfection, and served hot!" Oh yes, our palates are on fire…

Our buxom beauty showcases the world of Sam Nichols ("Cowboy Sam – The Old Cowhand From the Rio Grande"), a country comedian who sang about sex in a style "plumb loaded with the juices of life, love, and seduction to tickle your funniest bone". Sam's slow drawl, akin to the cartoon character Deputy Dawg, is endearing and addictive, and *Courtin' on a Mule* is a country comedy number sung atop some surreal electric steel guitar. As Sam sings: "You don't know what courtin' is till you've courted on a mule."

"I don't have to do this for a living," Sam tells us. "I can starve to death if I want to." And so on he goes courtin' a girl with "the prettiest blue eyes I ever did see, one blew this way and one blew that". Sam's song continues until his technique pays off, and our happy twosome ride off into the sunset with his girl holding tight on to his saddlebag.

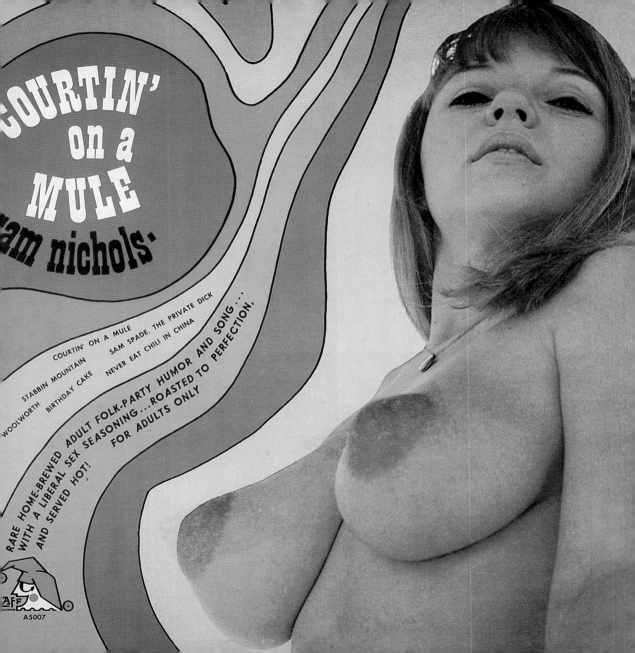

COURTIN' on a MULE

·am nichols·

COURTIN' ON A MULE

STABBIN MOUNTAIN   SAM SPADE, THE PRIVATE DICK

WOOLWORTH   BIRTHDAY CAKE   NEVER EAT CHILI IN CHINA

RARE HOME-BREWED ADULT FOLK-PARTY HUMOR AND SONG ·:·
WITH A LIBERAL SEX SEASONING...ROASTED TO PERFECTION.
AND SERVED HOT!.   FOR ADULTS ONLY

AFF
RECORDS

A5007

Rex Benson Strikes Again

A "downright lascivious" offering is how this record from Rex Benson is described, and if the knockout cover is anything to go by, this assessment can't be far wrong. Recorded live at the Largo club in Los Angeles, where Rex has long been a big draw, this record is said to be: "Guaranteed to keep you well aware of your funnybone and tie your spleen in knots." Rex is a caring man and worries about us all: "Very few people laugh today. There are so many pressures in society that nobody knows how to have fun any more." He tries to cheer us up with a few jokes and manages a rapid-fire run of goodies that do the job just fine. "It's tough being a star," he tells us, and despite a favourable write-up in *Christian Science Monitor*, he still worries about the crowd's reaction: "'How come you're not laughing?' he asks one gentleman. 'I laughed when you came in.'"

REX BENSON STRIKES AGAIN

THE HOLE IN THIS RECORD
HAS A MEANING...BUT
THE RECORD IS DOWNRIGHT
LASCIVIOUS!!!

FOR ADULTS ONLY

RECORDED LIVE AT:

CHUCK LANDIS' LARGO

LAFF RECORDS

LAFF A5020

Sex Menu Internationale

Could this blonde have been photographed in the depths of a forest in Sweden, Denmark, or Norway?
With the topless imagery now proclaimed to be "frameable cover art", we might be forgiven for thinking that we could be in line for a tasty piece of Scandinavian erotica, but sadly *Sex Menu Internationale*, cover excluded, just fails to deliver.

Provocatively titled as "ribald, United-Nations-styled delights", which conjure up thoughts of exotic orgies with girls of all ethnicities and untold opportunities for multilinguicity, instead what we get is a real let-down. This is a radio play, set in the United Nations building at the "heart of New York", that's neither sexy nor particularly international. We did think of sending the record back for a refund but, having sadly been defunct for some time, we guess Laff had the last laugh with this one. Our only recourse is to the European Court of Human Rights – we'll keep you posted.

Sex menu
Internationale

RIBALD, UNITED-NATIONS-
STYLED
DELIGHTS FOR THE PARTY
ALBUM GOURMET

FOR ADULTS ONLY
(FRAMEABLE COVER ART)

LAFF
RECORDS
A5002

Hollywood Up Tight!!!

Here we have a Hollywood flower-child living the hippy dream – she's certainly out of it on grass! – while adorning an album of less-than-subtle comedy from Tony Savone.

Tony brings us a "Hollywood orgy" from the "swish alps" with material that would be difficult to get away with today. While in the unreconstructed '60s era you might think that racist comedy would be the obvious comedy fallback, it's actually women and gays who tend to be the main targets here:

"I was walking down Hollywood Boulevard and two priests ran into each other. One of them said 'Hail Mary' and the other said 'Hi Nancy'."

"'Oh Henry, I'm going to have a baby.' 'Really Walter? Who's the father?' 'Silly, you think I've got eyes in the back of my head?'"

"You know what they call bloomers in Japan? Sackanookie!"

Tony Savone's material actually says as much about about the diversity of life in Hollywood as it does about any perceived deficiencies in his funnybone. And unlike the '50s nightclub comedy that has been featured, *Naked Vinyl* would never seek to endorse such cheap and tawdry observations on humankind's rich diversity – unless the pictures are good of course, and then, well, it's art...isn't it?

tony savone

A SALTY BAG OF LIVE, ASSORTED HOT HOLLYWOOD PARTY NUTS BY A FAST-PACED PARTY-MASTER.

hollywood up tight!!!

JEWISH ALPS
LYNCHING A FAGGOT
FROOT PICKING PEOPLE
SARAH SITS
NUDES STRIP POKER
SOUR NUTS
IN CHINA THEY DO IT FOR CHILI
THE ABCs OF SUBURBAN LIVING
EASY COME, EASY GO
THAT'S NO DIMPLE
RABBITS, RABBITS
THE LADY GOLFER
THE CAT DIED

LAFF
RECORDS
A-5021

FOR ADULTS ONLY

Undercover Safairi

Another natural setting – well, it is supposed to be a "safari", albeit this particular one seems more uncovered than undercover – and a camera angle and lens combination that appears to have enabled this girl's anatomy to defy gravity. Any more tree-hugging like this and it's our sap that will be rising.

"Bub" Thomas is another in a long line of blue comedians. He dubbed himself the head of the "National Association for the Promotion of White Trash" and had a sure touch with song – "She just turns her back and lays there cheek-to-cheek". He says he once lost a gas station job – "for pumping Ethyl…regular…". His material was a little more political and he had some good jokes, a classic line-up of saucy covers, and sleeve notes that tell Bub's story in an interesting and amusing way. As the man tells it, this record will "catch you right there where the gas gathers".

Pages 104-05: Well, if she's one of the "swizzlers and swingers", that reminds me – mine's a double and make it a stiff one…

ndercover safairi

by Bob Thomas

"MR. ENTERTAINMENT"

HAVE A GOOD TIME
THE DRUGSTORE
MY UNBORN SON
MEXICAN HOOTENANNY
THE SONG WRITER
BEATNICK
THE SAFARI

*A COCKTAIL CARAVAN
OF WILD ADULT
PARTY TALES AND TIDBITS*

(FRAMEABLE COVER ART)

LAFF
RECORDS

ULTS ONLY   A5009

the happy drunk !

by *Bub Thomas*

"MR. ENTERTAINMENT"

FACE THE MUSIC
ADVICE FROM THE PSYCHIATRIST
IT HAD TO BE ME
THE POLITICIAN
THE MOVIE BUSINESS
THE HAPPY DRUNK

CORKERS AND BOTTOM-OF-THE-BOTTLE BRANNIGANS, A SEX STORY COCKTAIL FOR SWIZZLERS AND SWINGERS

(FRAMEABLE COVER ART)

FOR ADULTS ONLY   A5008

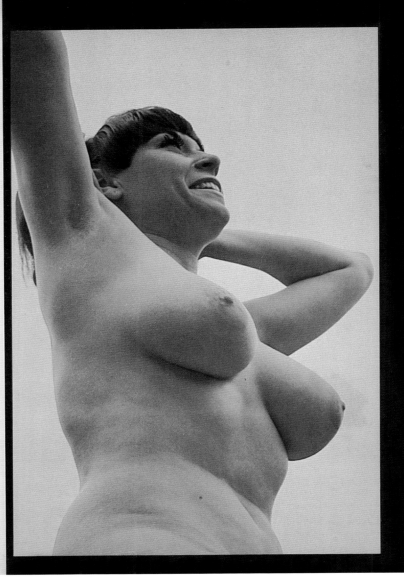

LIKE... DIS MUS' BE DA PLACE!

CRAZY COO-COO WEIRD

HIS BEATNICK IN KING ARTHUR'S COURT BLASTS CHASTITY BELTS!

"THE MONTANA SHEEP HERDER" COULD MAKE A EWE TURN!

HIS HILARIOUS *DRUNK* ROUTINES COST HIM $40,000.⁰⁰ TO MASTER ... (AT 50¢ PER SHOT!)

EVERY NIGHT NEW YEARS EVE!

"BUB" THOMAS

WAS BORN IN LEWISTOWN, MONTANA AT A VERY EARLY AGE.........
MOVED TO LONG BEACH, CALIF WHERE HE AMAZED TEACHERS WITH HIS STUPIDITY AND IGNORANCE. SHOWED ARTISTIC ABILITY DOODLING ON REST ROOM WALLS.....
WAS THE LAUTREC OF EDISON JR. HIGH SCHOOL.....
BUT WAS 'TOO LOOSE' AND TOO SHORT!

PAINTED THE MURINAL IN THE ORIGINAL "ROARING 20's".......
WHERE HE HAD THE MENSROOM CONCESSION.
WAS NOT PAID.......TOOK OVER THE JOINT...
NOW HAS HIS OWN MEN'S ROOM........

BECAME A MURDEROUS ENTERTAINER.. HELPED KILL VAUDEVILLE IN LEADING COAST NITE CLUBS.......
BUILT HIS OWN CLUB .... CLUBS YOU OVER THE HEAD WITH HIS MAD ONE MAN SHOW OF PARODIES, PUNS AND WELL WRITTEN AD LIBS.

DREW THOUSANDS OF SERVICE MEN IN THE HOLLYWOOD CANTEEN DURING WORLD WAR II ....

DRAWS CHARACTERS INTO HIS CLUB BY DRAWING THEIR CARICATURES FOR FREE........ SO THEY WILL LAUGH AT THE MATERIAL HE SPENT THIRTY YEARS STEALING..)

DON'T BE A DUMMY!

A DIFFERENT TYPE VENTRILOQUIST.. *THE DUMMY WORKS* **HIS** *HEAD!*

LOST GAS STATION JOB···· FOR PUMPING ETHYL... REGULAR...

STILL SUFFERING FROM SHOCK OF WORLD WAR TWO ———— (HE WAS NEARLY DRAFTED!!!) OUTSTANDING IN SHORT ARM INSPECTIONS........

A SATISFIED CUSTOMER

BAR FLY

AN' THIS AINT NO BULL!

LAFF RECORDS

LAFF RECORDS
1607 SOUTH LA CIENEGA BLVD.
LOS ANGELES, CALIFORNIA 90035

THE NOSTALGIA OF THIS RECORD WILL BRING YOU MANY LAUGHS..... BRING A TEAR TO YOUR EYE, A LUMP IN YOUR THROAT AND CATCH YOU RIGHT THERE WHERE THE GAS GATHERS....
GUARANTEED TO TRANSFORM YOUR HOME INTO A ROARING BAR!

RECORDED LIVE FROM THE STAGE OF THE ORIGINAL "ROARING 20's" 166TH & CRENSHAW TORRANCE CALIF.

5

The Laughter Machine

The era of the '50s and '60s was a hothouse for comedy and comic performances captured on record proliferated. The comedians of the day had jokes coming out of their ears – not all of them good – and the paying public were more than willing to laugh along.

Where did the jokes come from? "There are jokes everywhere and jokers eager to tell them and risqué humour in all sorts of ordinary situations," says Bert Henry, one of the stand-up stars of *Naked Vinyl*. He continues: "It takes a certain talent to be able to tell a joke well and make the audience see the pictures, particularly a risqué joke."

Bert was one of a motley crew of "blue" comedians – alongside others, such as Bob Thomas, Beryl Williams, Kenny Karol, and Stu Gilliam – whose material was funny and rude enough to remain popular but which didn't become offensive. This was crucial, because, at that time, if a comedian stepped over the perceived line of decency, the authorities could be quick to pounce. Lenny Bruce was one comic whose pores oozed "trouble" and the police watched him at every turn. The forces of law and order took umbrage at his vocabulary and humour, and it became a contest. Bruce was famously arrested for using the word "cunnilingus" on stage and he even made a record of his stage show to use in court to prove that the material was not obscene.

Though Bruce takes the prize for achieving the most notoriety, it was his fellow comedians who stole the march when it came to the risky and risqué album cover. And in deference to this alternative achievement we're going to concentrate on the tamer jokes told by the comedy stars of naked vinyl. But before you read them, close your eyes for a second, take yourself back to the '60s, and imagine a raucous audience in a smoke-filled

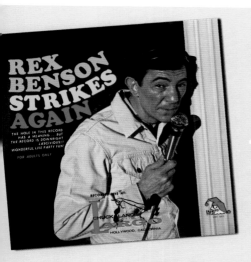

room, where the alcohol is flowing and the comedian is in full flight.

"My last girl she loved fur, she wore minks all day and fox all night."
Kenny Karol

"I've had five years of happy marriage, which isn't bad out of 15."
Beryl Williams

"My wife looked at me one night and said, 'Do you think I'll lose my looks when I'm old?' I said, 'if you're lucky'."
Beryl Williams

"My wife would have the last word with an echo."
Stu Gilliam

"On the way down I stopped in this bar and there's a good-looking girl there, and I said, 'honey, what time do you have to go home?' And she said, 'how much money have you got?' And I said, '$300' – and she said, 'not till next Friday'."

Bert Henry

Great Piano Pieces

We're proud now to present Hi In-fidelity Records, the jokers of *Naked Vinyl*'s pack, whose spoof albums came complete with a card disc insert bearing the legend: "I bought this Album for you as a gift...sorry, I couldn't afford the record!" On the backs of the covers were suggested song titles, specially chosen as comic takes on the record titles and themes.

Hi In-fidelity records were released on the mysterious Kanrom label and photographed by Ra Cantu. They were records to give as presents to the album-loving audiophile with a sense of humour.

Featuring an assortment of babes quite literally on piano, *Great Piano Pieces* has its classical styling complemented by the suggested tracks "Dizzy Fingers" and "It's A Grand Night for Swinging". It seems obvious what "Kitten on the Keys" refers to...and these particular kittens are definitely going to have you practising for your piano lesson all week long.

Pages 110–111: *Famous Cavalry Riding Songs* was about more than military expeditions on horseback – "Down In The Valley" was where the officers rode, dismounting occasionally for a foray further afield, as "Babes in the Wood" caught their eyes.

Pages 112–113: *Goddamn Great Drum Music*, sports more tom-toms than you can shake a drumstick at. While still managing to recall the night before, *Music for Hangovers* served up "Soused on the Border" and a song that the cover ladies seem happy to act out, "Belly up to the Bar, Boys".

Pages 114–115: *Songs for Swinging Mothers* is a genuinely witty pastiche of a Frank Sinatra classic (*Songs for Swinging Lovers*). "I Should Have Danced All Night" is the mothers' lament, while "I Didn't Know the Gun Was Loaded" sounds like a pretty lame excuse.

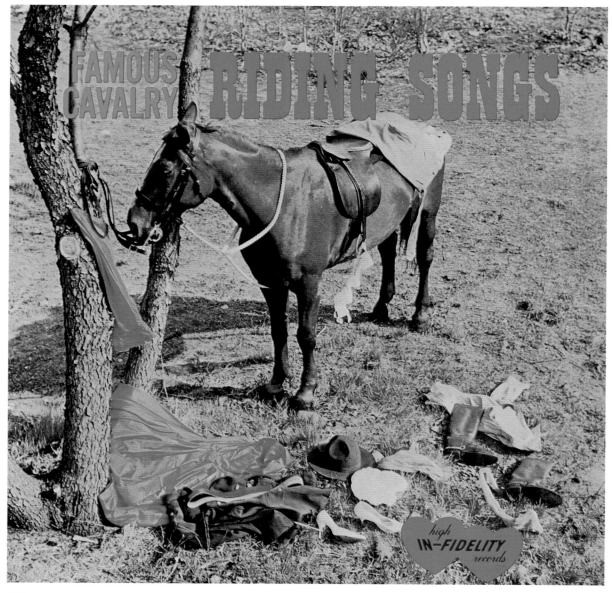

FAMOUS CAVALRY RIDING SONGS

high IN-FIDELITY records

FAMOUS CAVALRY
RIDING SONGS

Suggested titles, suitable for enclosure
in this Album Cover, are as follows:

Under The Yum Yum Tree
We'll Make Hay While The Sun Shines
Swingin' Down The Lane
Babes In The Wood
Captain Jinks Of The Horse Marines
Come Where My Love Lies Screaming
The Green Grass Grew All Around All Around
One For My Baby And One More For The Road
Back In The Saddle Again
Ridin' High
One O'clock Jump
Down In The Valley

high
IN-FIDELITY
records

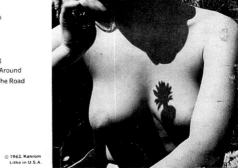

© 1963, Kanrom
Litho in U.S.A.

Goddamn
Great
Drum
Music

high
IN-FIDELITY
records

Cast Your Fate to the Wind

We move on now from the world of comedy, sex, and song to the more refined pleasures of musical entertainment.

Our next selection of records offers a place where the nude cover evokes the mood of the record it encloses, just as the music on record shapes the mood of the listener. These albums contain songs for the living-room stereo that while away the hours in the comfort of your own home. A relaxing record on the stereo, a hot, milky drink, and a nice snooze – that's what '60s culture was *really* all about.

In this vein Sounds Orchestral offers us orchestral interpretations of popular melodies packaged with a back-to-nature visual interpretation of Vince Guaraldi's hippy classic *Cast Your Fate to the Wind*, which enabled the listener to enjoy a taste of the hippy lifestyle without having to undergo the hassle of actually being near any hippies.

The cover offers us a perfect example of what we choose to call "the art of the subtle nipple" – an art form that with delicacy and skill allows an everyday glamour photo to become something altogether more erotic. Here the *modus operandi* is the silhouette, enabling the nipple in question to appear tantalizingly in the sunset and reflection.

Photographic perfection.

Hits of Today

It's time now for a little arty rug action, courtesy of 101 Strings and their label's abstract demonstration of the fully-naked, fur-lined recovery position. However, we feel there must have been some sort of communication breakdown between photographer, record company, and designer, because the cover image quite obviously works a lot better the other way round.

Musically, we're offered a lush selection of action, 101 Strings having decided that what's needed are some cover versions of the songs of Jim Webb and Burt Bacharach. In the process, we're given orchestral makeovers of "Galveston", "The Look of Love", and "Do You Know the Way to San Jose". By the time we got to "By the Time I Get to Phoenix", we appreciated the claims of the sleeve notes: "…much always depends upon interpretation and in the hands of the talented musicians who go to make up the 101 strings, Bacharach and Webb have found exactly the right partners." We couldn't agree with their agent more.

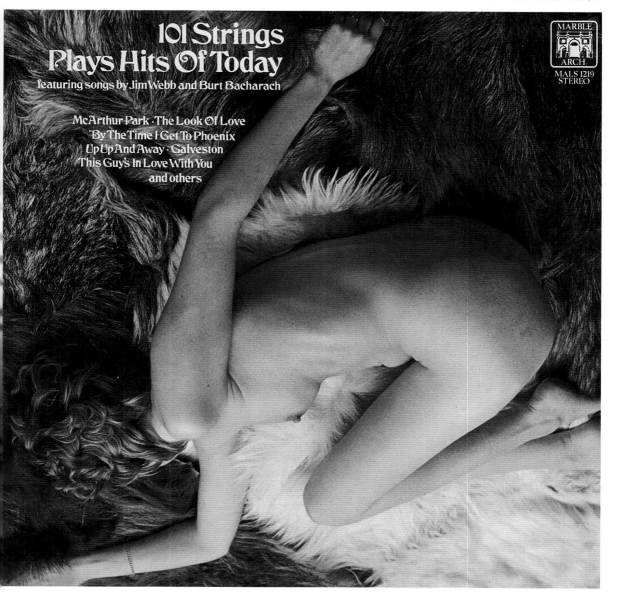

Bacharach Baroque

**As we all know, the '60s were a time for experi-
mentation; in this vein The 18th Century Corporation
brings us the songs of Burt Bacharach played on that
most psychadelic of instruments – the harpsichord.**
And by a minor miracle the mix of traditional instrument and
the gentle songs of Mr Bacharach create an album of
relaxing "olde worlde" charm.

If the idea had been developed it may even have given
Ravi Shankar and his sitar a run for their money, and an

18th-century Beatles would have added a little extra charm
to the decade. As for the cover, well, it depicts the life we'd
lead if we had half the chance! The bachanalian orgy more
than complements the theme of the album, as our happy
couple make love to the strains of "This Guy's In Love With
You", "Wishin' and Hopin'", and others.

All of course accompanied by the instrument of old. The
message of the album? Make hay while the sun shines,
preferably with a harpsichord playing in the background.

Bacharach Baroque

Played By THE 18th CENTURY CORPORATION

A dozen of **Burt Bacharach's** popular melodies including:
Do You Know The Way To San José–I Say A Little Prayer–Reach Out For Me–
Walk On By and This Guy's In Love With You

SUNSET

Love the One You're With

The Mystic Moods Orchestra was a musical phenomenon that sought to use the sounds of real life to create emotive music for the small hours. Created by audiophile, Brad Miller, the orchestra utilized "pioneering recording techniques" in an attempt to capture sound in as accurate a way as possible.

Originally inspired by the "sounds of the railroad", the Mystic Moods experience gradually expanded to include the sounds of the elements and the many moods of love. In their innovative and sometimes melancholy way they provided background music to the spiritual, philosophical, and sexual meanderings of a generation.

Their covers reflected this ethos and latterly came with erotic inner sleeves to suggest what the albums were really all about. As a soundtrack to romance, they're in a league of their own – albeit a slightly one-sided light orchestral league – and albums such as *Erogenous* and *Touch* smack of the sensuous aural delights on offer.

Love the One You're With was just such an album and it was originally released with plain cover and sexy inner sleeve, though we prefer the honest eroticism of this later edition. It begins with the sounds of a rainstorm and drifts through mellow orchestration, to a land of sultry pop classics played the Mystic Mood way. The rest of the album continues the theme, and from Jonh Lennon's "Love" to Bob Dylan's "Lay Lady Lay", we're lulled, hopefully with an acquiescent partner in tow, into a blissful romantic stupor. It's all about love, baby, and Mystic Moods provides the soundtrack.

Love the one you're with

Mystic Moods

Santo & Johnny Volume 4

Our cover lady offers proof that all that glitters sometimes *is* gold. Santo and Johnny were two brothers from Brooklyn, New York City, with a nice turn in tunes packaged within some super sexy covers. Sleeves for Volumes 1, 2, and 3 became progressively saucier until they went all out with this full-frontal, big budget, shiny gold affair. The successful duo, with Santo playing steel guitar and Johnny on rhythm guitar, had become famous when the instrumental "Sleep Walk" topped the pop charts in 1959. They followed it up with some hit albums that featured their distinct guitar-led sound. This volume has their instrumental twangy guitar style to the fore as they play modern interpretations of classical favourites composed originally by Liszt, Chopin, Mozart, Beethoven, Vivaldi, and Schumann.

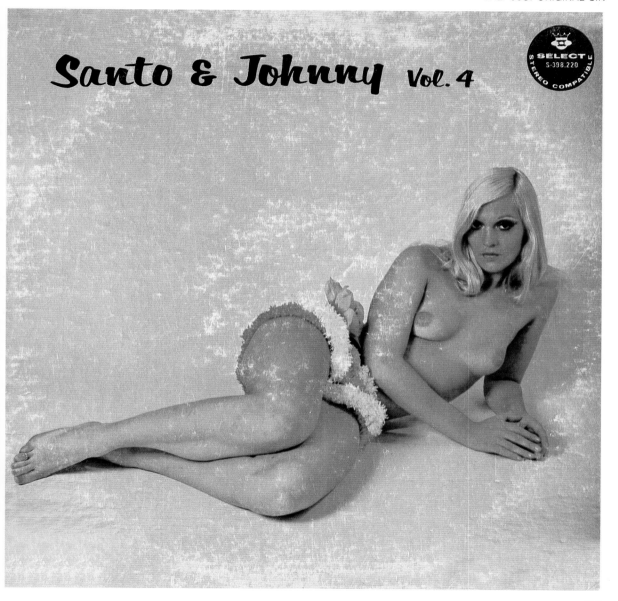

Santo & Johnny Vol. 4

SELECT
S-398.220
STEREO COMPATIBLE

Aphrodisia

Aphrodisia **brings us the sophistication of the "strange, mystic" East, along with a cover star who looks like she wants to be somewhere else – anywhere rather than posing for this shot; clearly, any aphrodisiac she had taken had worn off long ago.** Once recovered, our Eastern belle serves up authentic Afghan, Tadjik, Uzbek, and Turkmen music from lands where the "ancient cultures of the early ages live on", and as "strange, native, throbbing rhythms" take hold, we're told to expect to feel its aphrodisiac effects and be "swayed by its more earthly and primitive blandishments".

Music is undoubtedly many people's aphrodisiac of choice and you have to wonder if these records were ever slipped onto the stereo to add a touch of the exotic as couples advance towards the erotic. Although the public surely resorted to something a little more musically well-known, there must be anthropologists somehwere in the world whose love blossomed to the refrains of *Aphrodisia* – "Darling it's *Zurkhan*. They're playing our song". And if music be the food of love then *Naked Vinyl* is definitely the aperitif of choice.

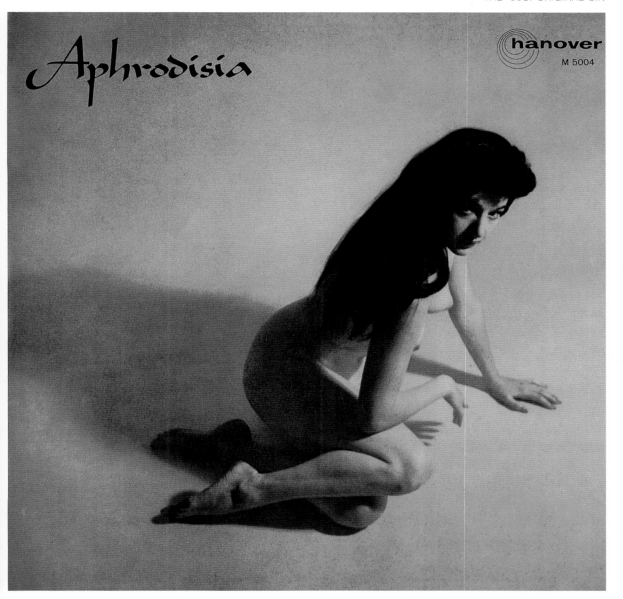

Aphrodisia

hanover
M 5004

¡Cubanga!

Caribbean music couldn't have found a more appropriate record label than Treasure, which brings us the "Torrid Latin Dances" of Cuba. This enables Treasure to treat us to a tasty, svelte Latina chick who must have had half of America desperate to jump on a plane to Havana, despite the little local difficulty of American-Cuban relations.

Teodoro Morales and his Latin Rhythmeers succeed in capturing Cuban rhythms in an authentic and enjoyable fashion, while we are spared the sleeve notes' synopsis of all things Cuban, in which it's safe to say the words "torrid", "passionate", "native", and "natural rhythm" would have featured prominently.

Cuban music encompasses many styles and this offering contains Mambo – a "fusion of Swing and Cuban music" – along with her Caribbean cousin the Merengue, plus the energetic Conga and the Cha-cha-cha. And not a mention of a cigar or a five-year plan.

TORRID LATIN DANCES

TEODORO MORALES
AND HIS LATIN RHYTHMEERS

TREASURE
TLP 806

HI-FIDELITY
RECORDING

¡CUBANGA!

cha-cha-cha   mambo

merengue   conga

Merengues! Merengues! Merengues!

The first of two super-sexy offerings from the Sounds of the Caribbean record label brings us the best in Caribbean dance and is illustrated by the world's shiniest woman with the hippest Afro hairdo, crouched alongside that essential instrument of sexual innuendo, the horn. The parent company Request Records followed up with the classic albums *Calypsos From Panama*, *Limbo Carnival*, and the mighty *Voodoo Drums of Le Gip*, but it never quite managed to find a record-breaking cover to replicate the majesty of its finest hour.

Merengues! Merengues! Merengues! is a collection of the best of the merengue, a dance that began in the Dominican Republic and Haiti before conquering "the dance halls, night clubs, and radio programs of the world". Sounds of the Caribbean, "sensitive to the public's demand", also offers a handy guide to the story behind each dance:

"Go! Dance *Merengue*" – "…with a pretty girl who has a gorgeous figure."

"Maria" – "Listen, Maria, I swear that my feelings for you are true love."

"Take Me into the Dark" – "You tell me that the light bothers you and you enjoy being in the dark."

"Maricutana" – "On a dark night, while I was fishing, a spider bit me and a wasp."

"Without Bass Drum" – "…it is not the real thing."

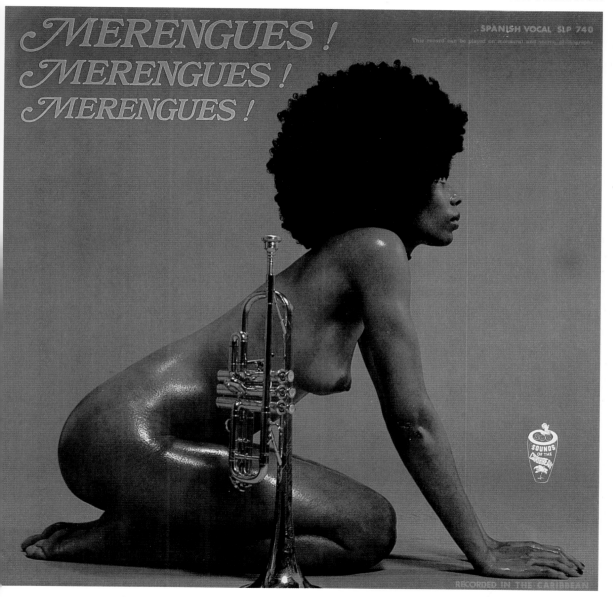

MERENGUES!
MERENGUES!
MERENGUES!

SPANISH VOCAL SLP 740
This record can be played on monaural and stereo phonographs

SOUNDS OF THE CARIBBEAN

RECORDED IN THE CARIBBEAN

Merengues Festival

Having "underestimated the public's love for the reborn dance", Sounds of the Caribbean was "forced by a flood of requests" to release a second album of merengues, again accompanying the song titles with helpful explanatory notes. We hope the feather-adorned hat hasn't passed you by, but if there is subtle symbolism on offer here, does the bird's less-than-perky condition carry any significance?

Still on the bird theme, we get the fantastic track "Little Parrot" ("She loved her parrot like a child") and a mysterious tribute to "Doc Jimenez" in the song "The Measles".

Also on offer are:

"*Merengue* is Like This" – "The Merengue is always danced with the girl one loves."

"Baseball *Merengue*" – "I like all the players."

"Give Me a Hand Gratey" – "A young man takes sick during a party, falls to the floor, and asks Gratey to help him back on his feet."

"Little Dolores…" – "so little but already has problems."

RECORDED IN THE CARIBBEAN

SPANISH VOCAL AND INSTRUMENTAL SLP 741
This record can be played on monaural and stereo phonographs

MERENGUES FESTIVAL

SOUNDS OF THE CARIBBEAN

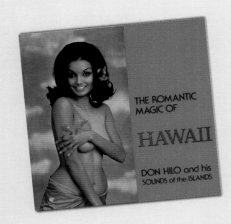

THE ROMANTIC
MAGIC OF

HAWAII

DON HILO and his
SOUNDS of the ISLANDS

Hawaii: An Island Paradise

Hawaii was the source of inspiration for so much of what you can see in *Naked Vinyl*. However, it was not just Hawaii that the music world fell in love with but every single island in the South Seas. And although we could have featured almost each and every one of them, we've chosen Hawaii because it, more than any other island, was the island that shaped American popular culture, including music.

Never ones to think small, Americans enjoyed their holidays in Hawaii so much that it was turned into a home from home when it became a state in 1959. Hawaii was thereafter a piece of America in the middle of the Pacific and Hawaiian culture, which had been influential for some time, went mainstream – a piece of the Pacific throughout America. From Hawaiian shirts to The Beach Boys and pineapple in a burger, Hawaiian culture was the height

of fashion – floral garlands as a form of greeting became famous worldwide and *Hawaii 5-0* made even the streets of San Francisco seem East Coast.

Hawaiian music's popularity stuck around for quite some time. In fact, Hawaiian output constitutes a large proportion of the backlist of "exotica". Audio Fidelity featured Hawaiian music prominently, while the hula girl has graced an incredible number of front covers, with quite a few of them represented here in the pages of *Naked Vinyl*.

Hawaii brought surfing to the world, courtesy of Olympic swimmer Duke Kahanamoku and surfing brought Elvis to Hawaii for his 1961 film *Blue Hawaii*. It really was a palm-tree paradise and everyone wanted to be there, singing Hawaiian songs to prove it. On-screen, Elvis even "married" Joan Blackman at Kauai's Coco Palms resort and returned in 1966 for *Paradise: Hawaiian Style*.

"Aloha! Welcome to the 'floating islands' – Hawaii, Maui, Oahu, Molokai, Kahoolawe, Kauai, Lanai, and Niihau. Come enjoy a glorious paradise warmed by a tropical sun, a world splashed with radiant colours enhanced by cobalt waters and gleaming white beaches." Audio Fidelity

To finish, we'll let Audio Fidelity sing the island's praises once more: "Here lovely maidens dance the *hula*, which they call 'the rhythm of life', accompanied by the strains of ukuleles and the pulsing rhythm of native drums. *Aloha* and *wikiwiki* ('hurry up!'). There is much to see, much to hear."

Siren Songs of the South Seas

This album of fine exotica from Pepe and her Rarotongans is adorned by a particularly alluring maiden – the track "*Te Mii Ne Au*" ("I Dream Of You") must have been written specially for her.

Other songs on the album range from the melancholy "*Ua Reva Ote Kaveka*" (Loved One That Went Away), to the sublime "*Aue Taku Tane*" (Oh My Love). Subtitled "Music of the Tropical Isles", such a beautiful mix of instruments and vocals – by Sony and Pepe – as this would have anyone swaying in the breeze.

There are themes that have meaning for us all, especially in respect of the cover girl – "*Moe Moea*" ("Dreaming") and, more disconcertingly, "*Eaa Toou Peka Peka Inapo*" ("What Was the Matter Last Night?"). After having admired *Siren Songs Of The South Seas*, you can see now why Gaugin spent so long painting the women of Tahiti.

Siren
Songs of the
South
Seas

6153

Music for a Belly Dancer

Our final offering in this field is a statuesque Middle Eastern affair from the ever-productive vinyl vaults of Audio Fidelity. The music is once again from the late Mohammed El-Bakkar, who succeeds in spanning three decades of coverage in *Naked Vinyl*, although by this stage he was somewhat vintage. The front cover declares it to be a "two record set" – and most of us could have guessed it is a double from the image alone. "Glorious Fatima" perhaps?

The claim made in the sleeve notes that belly dancing's impact in the West may be as profound as Arabic numerals offers evidence only that the writer had spent too long in the afternoon sun, but it cannot be denied that at times belly dancing was incredibly popular in America.

A stack of records were released featuring *Arabian Nights*-style music and covers, showcasing the delights of the female belly. When its appeal faded like many another dance fad, it did at least leave a legacy of incredibly well-toned housewives.

AUDIO
FIDELITY
AF

AF 2411
STEREO

TWO
RECORD SET
BELLY DANCE
MUSIC
AF

music
for a
belly
dancer

A Very British Affair

On the British side of the pond, sex was always a behind-closed-doors affair; it was done, but not too well, and it certainly wasn't talked about. But things began to change in the 1950s, and with the Profumo affair in the 1960s, when a government minister was discovered to be sharing a mistress with a Russian naval attaché, sex went public and things have hardly looked back.

The fabled reserve of repressed Britons was under attack. Although schoolboy humour had long been evident in sassy seaside postcards and the saucy *Carry On...* film series, in London's Soho district the overt action started to hot up and strip joints and adult shops boomed. Appropriately enough, one such establishment on a corner of Dean Street was built on the site of a mansion where King Charles II had kept one of his mistresses in the 17th century. Laws at the time were strict and stated that any woman nude on stage had to stand still when performing, but the owners of the strip joint circumvented this by turning the venue into a private members club called The Gargoyle Club, devoted to striptease and "blue" comedy.

With Carnaby Street on Soho's doorstep, sex and fashion were set to merge in a flash of British colour. As hemlines rose and Mary Quant's mini-skirt chic took the fashion world by storm, Britain, with The Beatles and The Rolling Stones, seemed to be the ultimate "with-it" place to be.

But when it came to sex on record, Britain remained true to type. Excess was out and big was not considered beautiful. British women made no attempt to keep up with their sisters in America, chest size-wise.

Like a British summer, the self-belief of the '60s didn't last long. It was back down to earth with a self-defeating,

pessimistic bump in the '70s. One difference was that sex was now firmly on the menu and the seductive glam of Roxy Music and their erotic covers featuring Jerry Hall pointed to a new era of cool for Britannia.

"My life has been one long descent into respectability."

Mandy Rice-Davis, friend of John Profumo's mistress, Christine Keeler

12ª raccolta

FAUSTO PAPETTI
SAY

3

The '70s:
Sunshine and Sex

Ferrante & Teicher

Whereas Americans are widely perceived to be effervescent and enthusiastic, exuberancy doesn't really figure much in most people's assessments of British character traits. British cover artwork follows this trend and could strike the impartial observer as being better suited to brightening up a wet weekday than setting one's passions and desires aflame.

The album opposite is a case in point. It features the Hollywood pianists Ferrante and Teicher, and was released on the budget British label Boulevard. Our two pianists (try saying that after you've had a drink) provide a little folk-inspired musical ambiance with rhapsodies that are "free-ranging in form and ebullient in style".

Somehow it seems appropriate that this first British record should feature grey skies, but if this is what we can expect to encounter on a sodden beach, then we can understand what's meant by "Cornish Rhapsody". It may be damp underfoot, but we can't complain about the view.

Pages 146–47: It takes a moment for you to realize the splendour of what you are staring at: the immense movement in unison, the glistening rocks, the rising and falling accompanied by such breathtaking noise…what natural splendour – the falls at Niagara truly are one of the wonders of the world, thoroughly deserving of such an honour as an album like this.

Ferrante & Teicher

Rhapsody in Blue
Rumanian Rhapsody
Cornish Rhapsody   Swedish Rhapsody
Hungarian Rhapsody No. 2
Hollywood Rhapsody

BOULEVARD

Million Sellers of the Sixties

Another Boulevard budget special, this time big-selling hits of the "sixties" sung by session singers in the early '70s. The album offers a collection of half-decent cover versions of the songs that "inspired us throughout 1967". And we get a selection of classic tracks that many can still hum decades later, from "(Sittin' on the) Dock of the Bay" to "Honky Tonk Woman".

The song-writing credits read like a who's-who of the great "soulful" writing duos, with tracks written by Jagger/Richards, Whitfield/Strong, Lennon/McCartney, Stevenson/Gaye, Cropper/Redding, and others, while the girl on the cover clearly leans towards the "San Francisco" scheme of things – long hair and love-ins. With body paint and beautiful model, surely this cover is enough to take even the most forgetful hippy back to the glorious summer of '67.

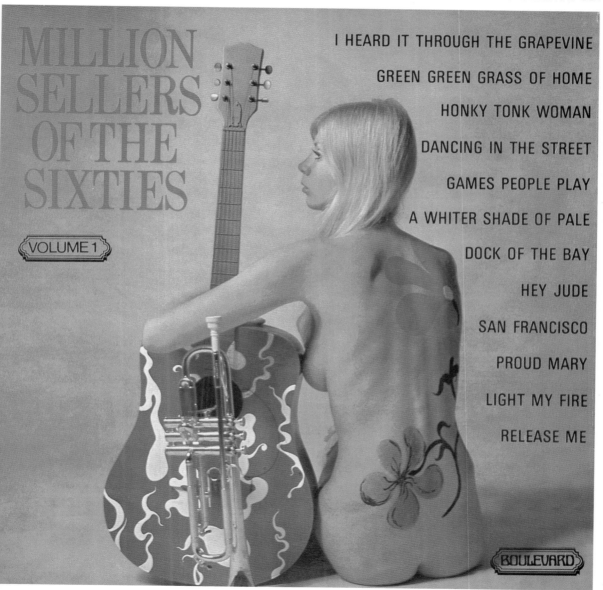

MILLION SELLERS OF THE SIXTIES

VOLUME 1

I HEARD IT THROUGH THE GRAPEVINE

GREEN GREEN GRASS OF HOME

HONKY TONK WOMAN

DANCING IN THE STREET

GAMES PEOPLE PLAY

A WHITER SHADE OF PALE

DOCK OF THE BAY

HEY JUDE

SAN FRANCISCO

PROUD MARY

LIGHT MY FIRE

RELEASE ME

BOULEVARD

Music for the Small Hours

Deacon was another cheap and cheerful British record label that saw fit to grace their covers with female nudity, with *Music for the Small Hours* providing us with this provocative flash of a nipple. Is it just us, or is she saying "and that's all you're getting!"

Alfred Scholz and his Silver Strings offer us "orchestral versions of popular melodies" – the standard fare of numerous '70s' budget releases. As we listen we are engrossed by the "deep-throated orchestra of strings and wood-wind" which provide a "pleasant and relaxing atmosphere". For small-hours seduction, we assume. Among these memorable tunes are "Dream A Little Dream", "Plaisir D' Amour", the "Breezes of May", and so many, many more – including "If I Didn't Care". As if...

THE SILVER STRINGS

play

Music for the
Small Hours

There's a Small Hotel
Dream a Little Dream
Before Another Spring
Last Letter Scene
Gondolier
Venus Waltz
Plaisir D'Amour
Dance Ballerina Dance
If I Didn't Care
Dream of Love
Breezes of May
Theme For a Starlet

DEACON
STEREO

Blues & Brass

Another saucy effort from Deacon, and this time it's the "exciting combination" of blues and brass, resulting in a nice mix of bluesy-jazz with some jazzy-blues thrown in for good measure! What does "a tremendous rhythm section", "a terrific instrumentalist", and "a great brass section" add up to? Why, it must be the "excitement which is Blues and Brass", not to mention a naked woman, of course! Now that *is* exciting.

Within this pinnacle piece of cover design, the "blues" of the title is rendered in nothing other than the colour blue, while the musical style that is the "blues", being a creation of the African-American community, is subtly implied by the image of a black woman holding a horn, which, as we probably all know, is one of the "brass" instruments.

This is a cover with as much symbolism as a Renaissance masterpiece…well, perhaps not quite. The track "Design Inspiration Blues" is unaccountably missing from the listing.

BLUES & BRASS

Basin Street Blues
Limehouse Blues
Little Brown Jug
Blues in the Night
5th Avenue Blues
When My Baby Walks Down the Street
Steamboat Blues
and others

ACON
REO

The Latin World of Stanley Black

This is another beautifully posed example of the art of the subtle nude, with nipple barely showing – and the sombrero and earring included to set the Latin scene. Evocative lighting is used to suggest a sun-drenched, siesta-inducing climate – and also to hide the fact that Decca have borrowed Deacon's studio for the day.

The Latin World of Stanley Black forms part of Decca's "World of" series – an institution during the '70s. Decca searched high and low in their quest to honour deserving recipients with a "World of" record and featured artists were as diverse as David Bowie, Vera Lynn, and the country dancers of Wales. The series was resolutely British but they did have the decency to include that legendary arranger/orchestra-leader Mantovani – and if that's not enough to excite, we don't know what is.

Inside this particular sleeve cover, the British composer Stanley Black ventured to bring us something culturally enriching in the form of his versions of favourite Latin classics. Although we get many a fine tune, it's the kind of Latin sound that could only have been created by a traditional British musician – more dance hall than Dominica.

THE LATIN WORLD OF STANLEY BLACK

oney
guapa
ruco de pernambuco
mingo
gle bird
breeze and I
tic samba
os muchachos
a
omparsa
eu tristesse (a felicidade)
a llanera

DECCA

SIDE 1.

Tony Bennett	The Good Life
Colin Blunstone	I Don't Believe In Miracles
Johnny Cash	If I Were A Carpenter
Vikki Carr	Where Do I Begin? (Love Story)
Manitas De Plata	Hommage A Ma Guitare
Percy Faith	Windmills of Your Mind

SIDE 2.

Aretha Franklin	If Ever I Would Leave You
Johnny Mathis	Moon River
Peter Nero	Summer Of '42
Peter Nero	We've Only Just Begun
Marty Robbins	By The Time I Get To Phoenix
Kilima Hawaiians	Song Of The Islands

HEAR THESE GREAT ARTISTS ON THEIR OWN WONDERFUL CBS RECORDS – AVAILABLE FROM YOUR LOCAL RECORD DEALER.

Tony Bennett	Tony's Greatest Hits	62821
Colin Blunstone	Ennismore	EPC 65278
Johnny Cash	Hello, I'm Johnny Cash	63796
Vikki Carr	Vikki Carr's Love Story	64425
Manitas De Plata	Hommages	EMB 31003
Aretha Franklin	Greatest Hits, Volume I	40-63064
Johnny Mathis	Love Is Blue	63301
Peter Nero	Summer Of '42	64790
Marty Robbins	Have I Told You Lately That I Love You	80176
Kilima Hawaiians	Farewell Hawaii	EMB 31010

This stereo record can be played on mono reproducers provided either a compatible or stereo cartridge wired for mono is fitted. Recent equipment may already be fitted with a suitable cartridge. If in doubt consult your dealer.

CBS is a Trademark of CBS, Inc., USA.
Interpak I by Shorewood Packaging Co. Ltd. England

CBS SPECIAL PRODUCTS
A Service of CBS Records   STEREO

Right: *Music to Bathe By* was released to advertise a bath foam called Ondine Bath Dew and the cover featured this trio of sea nymphs, aquatic temptresses who were said to lure mariners to a premature death. The cover draws on Romantic depictions of figures and scenes from classical mythology, thereby offering further evidence of the artistic pretensions of *Naked Vinyl*'s collection. *Music to Bathe By* is an album for bath-time sailors the world over.

MUSIC TO BATHE BY

ONDINE
BATH DEW

Special BAF Sounds

Minor British label BAF bring us here a winning mix of soul, ska, funk, and reggae, along with, for reasons known only to them, a nude, slightly mad-looking female cover star.

In their quest for the best sleeve notes possible, BAF inadvertently invented the text message: "…damn it – why not ask one of the CATS…to do it and B/4 I could pop the questions, Mr Patterson volunteered". The rest of the notes hint at what may have been the inspiration for the album – "There are an assortment of musicians and singers – cooking this 'Pot', and so it must be interesting". This may also explain why it took "4 years to put together". All-in-all there's a real Beatnik edge to Xtopha Konyils' sleeve notes.

Dig it daddio!

special BAF sounds

SWAN LAKE

WILLIAM TELL

F Volume 1

Various Artists

The Art of the Sleeve Note

Producing and marketing a record doesn't just involve cobbling together a few tunes and putting a pretty picture on the front cover. You also have to let the listening public know what they're letting themselves in for, and this all-important role is played by the sleeve note. Usually written with panache, and always fulsome in its praise for the artist concerned, the sleeve note and its requisite linguistic agility is an art form in itself.

You can deconstruct a sleeve note in many ways, but the fundamentals remain the same:

1. The artist concerned is the best in his or her field and will soon be widely accepted as a musical genius.
2. The record in question is groundbreaking and unlikely to be equalled for a generation to come.
3. Why use two words when you can say the same thing with ten.
4. The exclamation mark is king!

Written by John Schroeder, founder member of Sounds Orchestral, the sleeve notes to *Cast Your Fate To The Wind* are a *tour de force*. Mr Schroeder, turning from musician to wordsmith, tries to convince us that music was instrumental in the success of the Apollo moon landing. We'll let John take up the story from here: "Now that man stands on the brink of conquering space and almost has one foot on the moon itself, one is inclined, I feel, to forget many of the things on this earth that have indirectly helped him there. One of them is surely music 'for music is the food of life'." He concludes that "those who create it are as ambitious and progressive as any space programme", though it has to be pointed out that they take a few less risks in the process. Also, they do have gravity on their side – that said, we have seen some covers that suggest otherwise.

Here are a couple more masterly examples of the art:
Les Baxter, according to the sleeve note, wrote *La Femme* as a solution to the "absence of music dedicated to the woman eternal, in the modern 'pop' field". While of Frank Pourcel, who conducted the piece, we're told that "no musician achieves the mood of Paris and a woman as effectively as does Pourcel. Ecoutez!"

About Phil Moore's *Polynesian Paradise*, we learn that: "*Polynesian Paradise* is more than the pulsating pleasure of a musical trip around palm trees, warm ocean currents, coral reefs, and grass-skirted loveliness. It's a kiss-covered call to dip deep in the charm and the sounds of love from these floating islands and fairy-tale lands."

We're sure that you'd now agree that the writing of sleeve notes is a polished profession – one that we think is ripe for a revival...nearly forgot the exclamation mark!

"As timely as a holiday and as refreshing as an ocean cruise"

Hugo Winterhalter's *Wish You Were Here*

Stereo Action Goes Broadway

RCA brings us an off-the-shoulder, semi-nude musical extravaganza, with its tasty line in rock-chick fashion – hoped to be enough to induce a sparkle of interest in even a jaded record-buyer's eye.

On the disc we get "the excitement of percussion… fused with the brilliance of brass", showcasing RCA's brand spanking new "stereo action" – "the sound your eyes can follow" (see pages 172–73 for more on this), which serves to put all the other types of sound well and truly in the shade.

As for the music, instead of a "simple-minded noisefest" (sounds good to us), Dick Schory explores the "sonic possibilities of this rare group with delicacy and wit", and so successful was he that the "noisefest" became a "full-fledged soundfest". Now that's real progress.

RCA

STEREO ACTION

THE SOUND
YOUR EYES
CAN FOLLOW

STEREO ACTION
GOES
BROADWAY

DICK SCHORY'S
PERCUSSION AND BRASS ENSEMBLE

Heat Wave • Seventy-Six Trombones • Keep-a-Hoppin'
Bali Ha'i • It's Legitimate • Slaughter on Tenth Avenue
Hernando's Hideaway • I Got Rhythm • Camelot • Show Me
The Sound of Music • El Sombrero

The Romantic Magic of Hawaii

With the merest hint of a Hawaiian nipple an ordinary cover is once more turned into a masterpiece of naked vinyl.

The Romantic Magic of Hawaii is a Damont production and Damont Records are one of the few smaller labels from the '70s that have survived the test of time, remaining to this day a pressing plant based in Hayes, Middlesex, England. The company was founded in 1972 by Dave Miller and Monty Presky (hence Damont) and throughout the '70s they sold thousands of 12-inch Stereo Gold Award (a fictitious marketing-inspired commendation) records in the UK for the princely sum of 49 pence (about 75 cents) each. Damont's best-sellers were an epic *German Beer Drinking Songs* album along with the soundtracks for *Star Wars* and *Close Encounters of the Third Kind*, both performed by the London Philharmonic Orchestra.

The subtitle of this Damont album is "Don Hilo and his Sounds of the Islands", a "musical passport to a land of gentle breezes and swaying palm trees". The don and his islander chums were in fact session musicians, and for these studio recordings a suitable name for each ensemble would be "pulled out of a hat", though we would like to think that a real Don Hilo exists somewhere on a South Seas island.

Monty Presky and friend

THE ROMANTIC MAGIC OF

HAWAII

DON HILO and his SOUNDS of the ISLANDS

Sounds Astounding

This equally alluring Damont effort offers us stereo twins in full space-age outfits – minus the airtight suits, of course – like extras from *Barbarella*. The synthesizer music seems the natural accompaniment for such a futuristic package.

Sounds Astounding features "speaker to speaker interplay of specially scored orchestral works with scintillating sounds augmented by synthesizers". Enough, surely, to please even the most discerning record buyer. Orchestras in the '70s often experimented with technology, and with the "astounding" effects wrought on *Sounds Astounding*, the listener got the impression of being transported into a brave new sonic future. This aural "trip" was made possible by the London Philharmonic Orchestra, with its "March of the Synthesizers", together with epic renditions of *Star Wars*, *Close Encounters of the Third Kind*, and *2001: A Space Odyssey*, all immeasurably enriched by the addition of electronic bleeps.

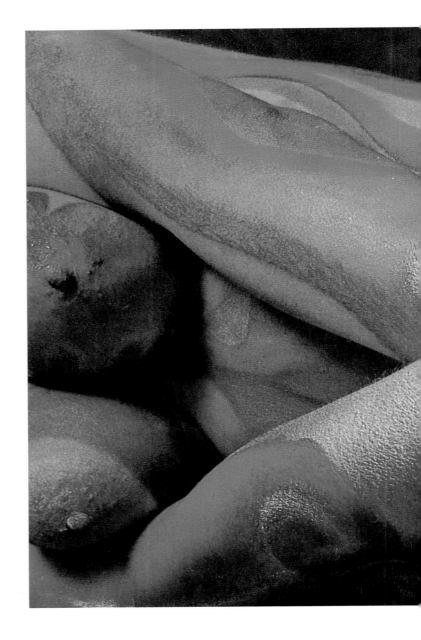

Right: *Child of Light* by Swegas – a British rock group that you might think was powered purely by sexual energy. The album as a whole is a perfect example of '70s rock excess. From the jazz-rock fusion of the music, to the cover's demonstration of face painting gone made, you've gotta love it!

Child Of Light · by 𝕾𝔴𝔢𝔤𝔞𝔯

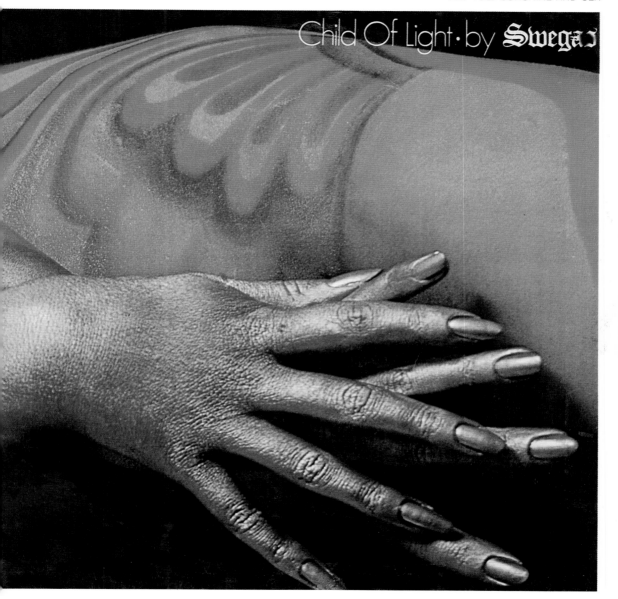

The Power of Stereo

The first stereo record was released in 1958 and it gave music a new lease of life, which today remains the unrivalled form of recorded sound. Changes to album cover art signalled this landmark innovation visually. The most popular choice was abstract designs using eye-catching typography, but equally eye-catching for the rest of us was the nude cover, which also attracted executive support because it sold the records while at the same time offering a still relatively new idea that lent an appropriately fresh and fancy look to the new stereo sound. From that moment onwards there was an accumulation of naked vinyl and records neither looked nor sounded the same again.

At some unknown point it was decided that only certain types of music were worthy of the new technology's moniker and these were released as specially produced stereo records. Most of these were classical, exotic, or electronic. The exotic music was felt to offer a rich sound range that stereo would bring out the best in, while for similar reasons classical music had the instrumental scope to demonstrate stereo's new-found wonders to full effect. Electronic music was the novelty act in this partnership – stereo was new and electronic music was new, so it was decided to put them together and see what happened.

Audio Fidelity was the prime exponent of stereo exotica, which it used to showcase its late '50s innovation, the "stereodisc" – "a study in high-fidelity sound" in which "the elements or musicians on the recording will be reproduced in the exact locations directionally, as at the original performance". If that makes sense to you, you will understand why they had to include the crucial upper frequencies that "may not be within the range of human hearing". Rather tough on man's best friend you might think.

RCA's "stereo action" series was "the sound your eyes can follow: the concept of music in motion, of sound in

space". Their new style of intelligent stereo meant that "the instruments seem to hover, wander, or flit between your two stereo speakers creating a musical experience entirely new in the world of sound". Before recreational drugs were commonplace, the allure of such effects proved an unsurprisingly popular aural experience. *Stereo Action Goes Broadway* was recorded live at the Orchestra Hall in Chicago. Special microphones were used to capture the "sonic 'feel' of the great hall", while a shiny nude cover was used to capture the sonic ring of cash registers nationwide. The combination had proved to be a winning one.

Stereo has ruled the world ever since and seems likely to remain unchallenged, unless perhaps quadraphonic makes a comeback or a new dimension in sound is discovered.

World Hits

This greatest hits album is the last of the British efforts being featured – while we know the British are supposed to be kind to their animals, this is surely taking things a little too far!

As a budget release this record is a *tour de force*. The listener is bombarded with rock cover versions of "songs made famous by international artists". Neither woman nor horse appear to link in any way to the 14 tracks, but that's sometimes the price you pay for getting a beautiful naked female on to the front.

Who's complaining though? Certainly not the happily nibbling nag.

WORLD from England's Hits

EL 1

ELASTIC

RECORDED IN ENGLAND
14 GREATEST SELECTIONS
SCHOOLS OUT
SEASIDE SHUFFLE
BREAKING UP IS HARD TO DO
POPCORN
IT'S FOUR IN THE MORNING
RUN TO ME
THE LOCOMOTION
ALL THE YOUNG DUDES
YOU WEAR IT WELL
LAYLA
TOO BUSY THINKING ABOUT MY BABY
WHERE IS THE LOVE
HURTING EACH OTHER
THE LION SLEEPS TONIGHT

What Now My Love

Sun, sea, surf, sex, the Hammond organ – can you spot the odd one out? The incongruity was, apparently, not quite so obvious in the '70s. While "playing on your organ" certainly offers a rather obvious smutty innuendo, this desire for sophisticated humour wasn't the reason for the sudden vogue of the portable electronic Hammond organ.

But what was? It has been said that it is the easiest instrument on which to fake it – one's playing talents that is. Whether true or not, there were keyboard players of great talent, and a number of groups arose that were based around them. Sadly, it isn't any of those that feature here; instead, a series of (other) organ-players – sorry! – sold a string of albums of this previously almost unshiftable music (well, let's call it niche) by virtue of the sexy covers. Stef Meeder, Jaap Zeeland, Klaus Wunderlich, Otto Weiss, Harry Stoneham, and many others produced a seemingly endless supply of three-minute Hammond medleys. If he is saying to her "What now my love?" – and the men can guess what he has planned – then it's a fair bet that she is thinking "Here it comes again"… and not in a welcoming tone.

Pages 178-79: *Little Things* indeed. We think the staff at Gemini Records had a one-track mind and myopia, while Stef – is it pronounced "stiff"? – managed to fit 60 tracks into 20 medleys over four sides, which is surely some kind of record.

little
things

STEF
MEEDER

Memories Are Made of This

Stef Meeder must have been a nice man – he seems to have loaned a photograph to his friend Jaap Zeeland, and it strikes us as a contender for one of the best in the series. Just what friends are for!

Jaap stuck with the same winning formula of a (stunning) nude cover and more Hammond medleys, such as the highly appropriate title song, as well as "Freight Train", "I Want to Be Happy", and of course the ever-popular "Time to Go". We know and love them all.

The appeal of the Hammond duly waned, partly in favour of the Moog synthesizer. A mysterious transfer of affection because the Moog couldn't play chords and wasn't exactly compact. My, how things have changed. Try persuading any of these cover girls that smaller can be infinitely better!

MEMORIES
ARE
MADE
OF THIS

JAAP
ZEELAND

Twice As Nice

Another Hammond organist was Otto Weiss, whose name happened to offer easier rhyming potential than those of his rivals – and here, of course, it scans with "twice as nice", thus providing the perfect pretext for a classic nude cover. You might also gaze longingly at the beach girl and remark "nice", twice.

Otto released a series of albums and was even dubbed "Mr Hammond" – a title that a few of the other lovers of the instrument may have contested. Especially as the alternative Mr Organ, just didn't have the same ring about it.

Otto also released an album called *At It Again*, which would surely have made for an equally spectacular cover in naked vinyl vein, though sadly it wasn't to be. Musically, Otto goes for a range of medleys from the Foxtrot to the Bossa Nova and the Pasodoble, which all help *Twice As Nice* to stand up as a work of Hammond mastery.

Twice as nice · Otto Weiss

JOY
SPECIAL

JS 5017/8

The Strip Goes On

Europe wasn't just about the Hammond medley. Other artists developed an upbeat, easy-listening style that every now and then called for a nude touch of class to enliven the proceedings.

One such example was Werner Müller's epic *The Strip Goes On*, which came complete with a fräulein on the cover – the summits of her twin peaks adorned with the national flags of, presumably, those who have conquered this inviting but forbidding edifice. The American did well, but the Briton seems to have failed to progress beyond the lower reaches…

This is a bizarre concept album themed on the world of stripping. As such we get cover versions of "The Stripper", "Satisfaction", "Rumba Juanita", and "Get Up, I Feel Like Being A Sex Machine". These classics are prefaced by Werner's own composition, "Bodybuilding", which is the soundtrack of a night at a strip club – as a couple look on in fascination at a male stripper, a conversation between the couple is set against swinging '60s nightclub music:

He: "Oh what a body."
She: "Oh what a man."
He: "He's ridiculous."
She: "He's wonderful."
He: "I hate it."
She: "I love it."
He: "He's an idiot."
She: "Lovely boy."
He: "That's unfair."
She: "He's a dream."
He: "Exhibitionist."
She: "Oh my sweet gangster."

"Oh Baby It's Cold Outside" but suddenly I feel I need some fresh air…

the strip goes on

Orchester Werner Müller

Too Darn Hot
Femme Femme
The Beat Goes On
Je t'aime . . . moi non plus
The Stripper
Oh Baby It's Cold Outside
Satisfaction
Get Up I Feel Like Being
A Sex Machine

DECCA

Chakachas

You may recognize our cover star from the earlier album *Merengues! Merengues! Merengues!* and she comes to us this time courtesy of the hippy-funk sounds of Chakachas. As she gives us the eye in sultry fashion, we're left to listen to an album packed with funky drumbreaks, soulful vocals, and brass flourishes.

Chakachas' sound has a tinge of afro-funk – that's African funk rather than a style befitting her hairdo! – and Latin and European cheese.

The album begins with well-known funker "Stories" and continues through the sing-a-long "Push Together", to the African tinged "Bantu", and on to the dyslexic "Copakabana"

It's funk for the easy-listening masses who like a nice tune to hum, along with the occasional good groove. As for Afros, well they're creeping back into fashion and it's surely only a matter of time before they once again rule the world.

Personally, we can't wait!

STORIES . PUSH TOGETHER . PARTY . CHAKACHAS JUDAS KISS...

Groove Grease

This record title is about as rude as it gets, being Philadelphian Jimmy McGriff's play on American sexual slang. The studio portrait composition makes good use of soft lighting to highlight points of interest for the viewer.

Jimmy McGriff's super-funky American Hammond grooves are more than an ocean away from the organ medleys of the Europeans; instead, they follow in the illustrious footsteps of

Bill Doggett and Jimmy Smith. Sonny Lester's sleeve notes report how McGriff's "attraction for the organ became a love affair and, happily, became the vehicle for McGriff's meteoric rise to Stardom". Here we have his "funky bag", and "influenced and encouraged" by Jimmy Smith, McGriff – "wizard of the jazz organ" – has produced many a fine Hammond album, and, of course, cover.

GM 503

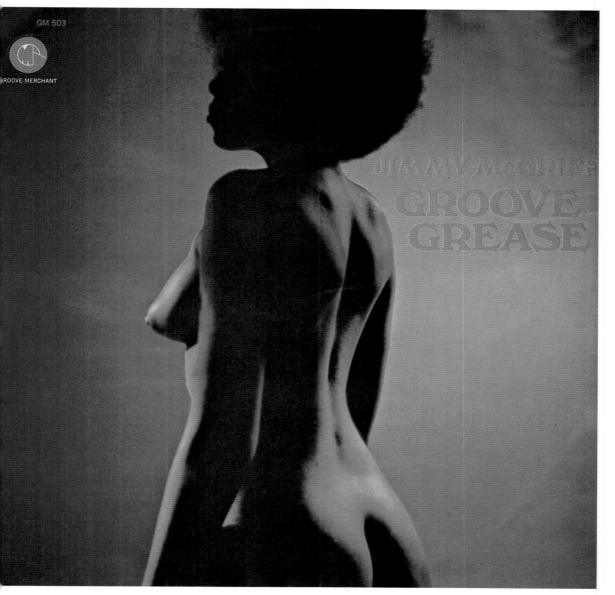

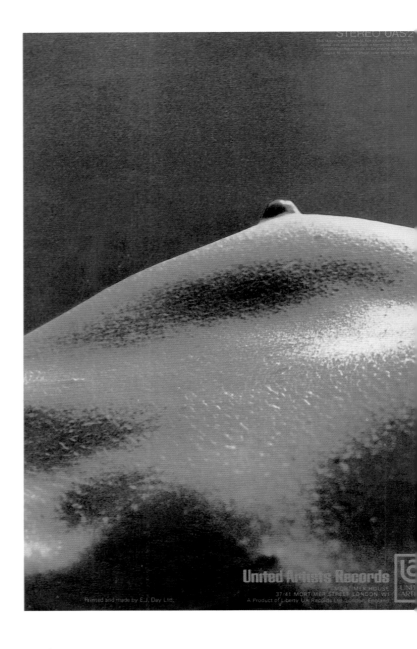

Right: Real art forms the cover of *Cochise*, using a clever juxtaposition of elements, and the subtle use of light and colour to capture the beauty of a rolling vista – a delectable landscape inviting you to explore further. Could there be a better suited opening track than "Velvet Mountain"?

Pages 192–93: For a change, our next two covers aren't voyeuristic or pornographic, or even really about sex as such; instead, they are more New Age metaphors for creation and life. The two covers – *All Things Beautiful* and *Just Family* – might almost be before and after affairs, with the beauty of womankind and her gift of fertility, to be able to reproduce in an otherwise barren world.

COCHISE

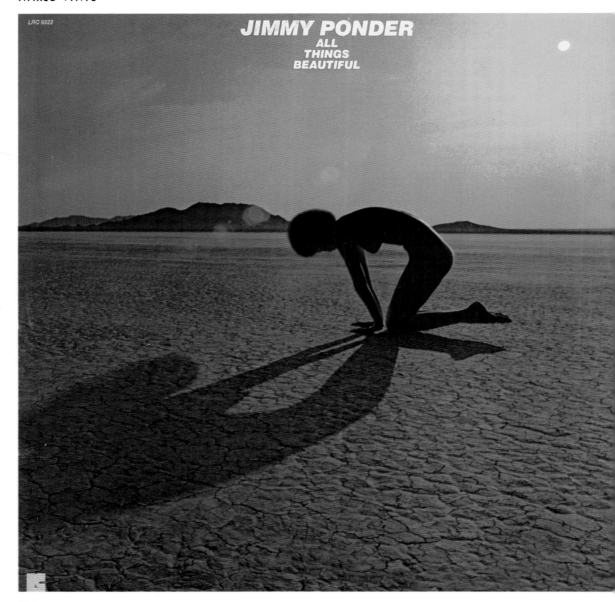

JIMMY PONDER
ALL
THINGS
BEAUTIFUL

LRC 9322

dee dee bridgewater

just family

Disco Daze

Disco music has often focused on sex, so it's not a surprise that it took naked vinyl to its sequined heart. However, it is ironic that what was originally largely a gay movement managed to provide further inspiration for graphic portrayals of the female form. Perhaps, though, this was just an inevitable part of disco's evolution into the mainstream, and as the songs became hits, and the style more European, disco became enmeshed with female fashion.

Born in the nightclubs and fathered by DJs, many of whom later become stars, disco music has a long history. As a movement, disco spawned both talent and tantrums, and brought glamour and wealth to the packed dancefloors of New York clubs such as The Loft, The Gallery, and later the celebrity-led Studio 54. As disco's popularity spread, the number of clubs mushroomed and eventually its influence was felt far beyond the confines of New York's coolest musical establishments – disco went global.

In its early days, disco developed a cult following, all bent on enjoying an eclectic assortment of music from Funk and Funk-tinged rock, to Soul, Latin, Afro-funk and beyond. The music provided a 'panoply of rhythms or an indigo mood'. The heady atmosphere that the scene created continued to thrive until money began to exert its distorting and tacky effect. With the involvement of the big record labels, disco made it on to the radio station airwaves

"People would come dressed in 'full funk regalia' (afros, 'nik nik' shirts, applejacks, etc.) and dance/mingle till the wee hours of the morning." David Leifer

and then into the charts. From around 1976 onwards disco was mainstream, and from the classic disco-pop of Chic, The Trammps, and Earth, Wind, and Fire to the camp of the Village People, it sold by the truckload. The death of disco has been mourned many times but the movement had had a good run for its money – a solid decade of success – and as an outlet for frustration in what was a rough era economically, it proved invaluably uplifting for many people. Towards the end of the '70s, *Saturday Night Fever* signalled the turbulent times ahead, not only for disco but for the entire entertainment business and fashion industry. Like the decade it decorated, disco was almost spent.

Of all the musical forms covered within this book, disco was the one that most inspired nudity. For example, Grace Jones would entertain the crowds at Studio 54 by turning up naked at every possible opportunity, while Jerry Hall pulled the same stunt once on horseback. The disco records we present here don't make any great claims to musical acclaim and this is perhaps why they feature nudes – to help sell the undistinguished music. But the covers are fantastic! As the modern revival in disco's fortunes shows no signs of abating, we bring you a little sip of her saucy past to savour.

"As a movement, disco spawned both talent and tantrums and brought glamour and wealth to the packed dancefloors of New York's clubs"

Discotheque Volume 2

Silver Convention was a trio of disco babes that brought a sexy disco vibe to the world, along with the best advert for sado-masochism that we've seen.

Their covers come in a long line of funky disco smut, from the steamy mid-'70s affairs of the Ohio Players to the super-sexy world of Salsoul. But it was Silver Convention that laid the disco cover bare and that's why the band graces our pages.

Discotheque Volume 2 features Silver Convention's biggest hit, the momentous "Get Up and Boogie". The come-on message in their songs is writ large, issuing a seemingly direct challenge to male sexual domination.

Of the songs on the album, "No, No Joe" suggests it will be when she's ready, while woe betide Joe if he can't keep it going when the answer is yes, with "You've Turned Me On (But You Can't Turn Me Off)". "You've Got What it Takes (To Please Your Woman)" is pretty much what any man would regard as music to his ears, while "Play Me Like A Yoyo" is the sort of invitation that's difficult to resist.

Page 198: Easy to recognize by the bondage trademark, Silver Convention once more bring a sexy disco vibe to the world with the album *Save Me*. These cuffs must be the "Chains of Love" – and who wouldn't want to be tied up next to a captivating view like that?

Page 199: Talking of ideal locations, what a vista of perfection is laid out for your delectation on the cover of *Dance Skinsation* – it gives a whole new meaning to the phrase "heavenly bodies".

Silver Convention
DISCOTHEQUE VOLUME 2

CONTAINS THEIR
HIT SINGER
'GET UP
AND BOOGIE'

MAGNET RECORDS

Love and Kisses

Love and Kisses brings us the original disco Lady Godiva – a cover that was surely inspired by Jerry Hall's infamous entrance to Studio 54 – nude on horseback.

You may notice that our bareback rider has had her nipples airbrushed out. Which is strange, we think you'll agree. While on record, side B offers us "Beauty And The Beast", which makes a lot more sense.

The record was released courtesy of the Casablanca Record and FilmWorks Inc., the outfit that gave the world the Village People and *Thank God it's Friday*, a *Saturday Night Fever*-style comedy. Buried at the bottom of the album credits is the enigmatic line "Special thanks to: the birds of paris". What do they mean? "Birds" as in women? "Paris" as in the capital city of France? The musicians were conducted by Jean Claude Petit, so who knows…

HOW MUCH, HOW MUCH   I LOVE YOU

love and kisses

Right: Pretentious hi-tech hi-fi sexuality from Space, the electronic "keyboards only" wizards whose gimmick it was to dress up like spacemen. Here they let their imaginations run wild with an interpretation of the classic Bowie alien blockbuster, *The Man Who Fell to Earth*. You're not going out (un)dressed like that, surely?

LDA 20317

SPACE
DELIVERANCE

Vogue

Cerrone's Paradise

Jean-Marc Cerrone, who seems to keep his dumplings on top of the refrigerator, lets us into a little corner of his fevered imagination with this none-too-subtle fantasy, an hour-long slice of low-down dirty disco.

Cerrone was the crown-prince of Eurodisco, contemporary to Bellote and Morodier and famous for the epic song "Supernature". He liked to spice up his songs with a bit of saucy chat and *Paradise* begins with three ladies waiting to see him live, during which they discuss the merits of, well, none other than Cerrone himself. We will let them tell you more:

"So girls, tonight's the night, sure is; it's cold out here, sure is, and I got my low-cut dress on too. This dress is especially for Cerrone, honey. Cerrone, oh my, he's fantastic; god, when I see him, what I could do to that guy. This lady at the door – can you help us?"

"I ain't gonna help any of you girls. Cerrone is mine. You can come and watch him, but hands off."

"We'll see who's gonna get there first!"

And he just looks like such a love god that you can readily understand what they're fighting over…there's hope for many of us yet, it seems.

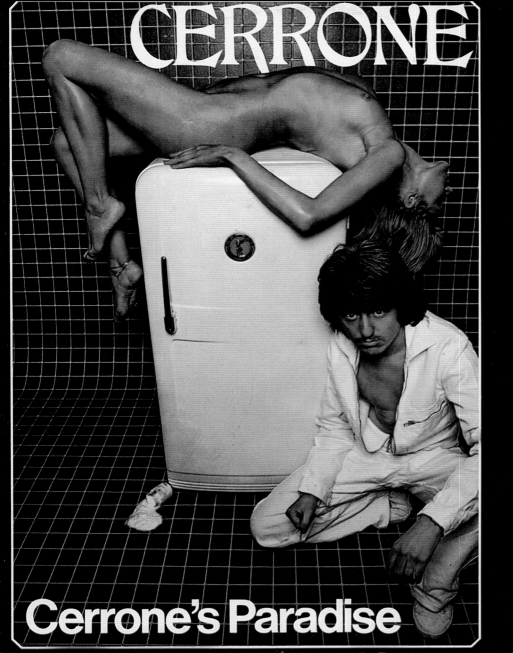

CERRONE

Cerrone's Paradise

Malligator

A Brief History of Breastaphilia

In case you had overlooked the fact, breasts have been around for a while now. Over the centuries a considerable vulgar vocabulary has developed in most languages, providing us with a rich lexicon of words and euphemisms for the bountiful and beautiful bosom. And it gives us considerable pleasure to be able to share with you some of the knowledge of this subject that we have acquired over the years.

There is an early example of this breast-obsessed linguistic creativity from the 17th century, when the word "apples" entered popular parlance – appropriately, this reference harked back to the garden of Eden and what you might think of as "the forbidden fruit". Look but do not touch. First ideas often prove to be the best, and it is another piece of 17th-century slang – "tits" – that has stood the test of time better that any other word for breasts. It is interesting to note, well for some of us at least, that "tits" derives from "teets", which was originally

a reference to nipples. Only over the course of time has the word assumed its modern meaning of the entire pair of breasts. The actual purpose of breasts lies behind the 18th-century use of "dumplings" and "dairies", emphasizing the wholesome delights of a natural food source. ("Baby's public house" was a later expression playing on the same theme and revealing the public's taste for a tipple.)

Rhyming slang introduced a whole new range of cunning linguals – if you'll pardon the expression. During the Victorian period there were the quaint "cabman's rests" and "threepenny bits" along with the more industrial-sounding "buffers". There was phenomenal scientific and technological advancement in this era and when this was coupled with a profound cultural appreciation of the arts, new expressions such as the statuesque "nature's founts" or the anatomically askew "top buttocks" were brought into being. Not to be outdone, the Victorian literati

"During the Victorian period there were the quaint 'cabman's rests' and 'threepenny bits' along with the more industrial-sounding 'buffers'".

conveyed their passion for an artistic eyeful by use of the word "charms" or the more poetic "cupid's kettledrums".

In modern times these wholly natural (outside California, at least) spheres of serenity have been christened time and time again, revealing that the linguistic dexterity of English knows no bounds – or perhaps it betrays our obsession. Whichever, we now have "baby bumpers" and "bazongas", the musical rhythms of "bongos" and "maracas", the fruity "melons" and "mangoes", the ever-popular "knockers", the automotive "honkers" and "hooters", and the streetwise "lobs", "shoulder boulders", and "jugs". As for nipples, from the "tits" or "teets" of the 17th century we have now progressed, if that's the word, to "cherries" and "kittens noses". Such is the inventiveness – not to mention the fixation – of 21st-century man.

Ivory

As lands of sporting heroes, sheep, movies, and movie stars, Australasia's reputation in the world of musical creativity isn't quite as superlative as some of its other achievements. Although there has been some great music out of the Antipodes over the years – most people would quickly think of INXS, the classic "Down Under" by Men At Work, Nick Cave, and, of course, Kylie Minogue – Australasia is featured here not for musical merit but for its expert eye in the art of erotic album cover design.

These covers are normally suburban and sunny, a cross between the American stag party scene and a soft-porn magazine. They serve up sexy entertainment to while away balmy evenings – little pieces of erotica for the boy and girl next door – and we think they're just fine.

Here Ivory demonstrate that a girl's best friend isn't necessarily a diamond, as they cleverly present themselves centre stage with an elephant-tusk equivalent of the Kohinoor diamond.

Side One
CELEBRATE
DON'T LET GO
I'LL GIVE ANYTHING
TIMES
SHOW ME HOW REAL YOUR LOVE IS

Produced by Robert John Lange
Featuring Albie Donnelly
Compiled by Laurie Dunn
Sleeve design by Peter Guild
Front cover photography Cooke-Key
Back cover photography Murray Close

℗ 1978 Virgin Records, Ltd., England
Manufactured and distributed under license by Festival
Records Pty Limited, Australia (London
Trademark owned by Virgin Records Ltd London
England and used by Festival Records Pty Limited
under authorization.

Side Two
I THINK I'M GONNA FALL (IN LOVE)
RIP IT OFF
GIVE IT THE NASTY

Right: Aussie rock group Supercharge
with *I Think I'm Gonna Fall (in Love)*
brings us another dreamy Australian
cover complete with blonde asleep,
foetal-style, stuck to a piece of glass.

Pages 212–13: *Disco-Gold* is another
sexy effort from Down Under, courtesy
of The Eddie Nelson Express, the group
that took disco to the Outback and
taught the menfolk of Darwin to stop
fighting and start loving.

L 36645
(V 2999)

SUPERCHARGE

I think I'm gonna fall (in love)

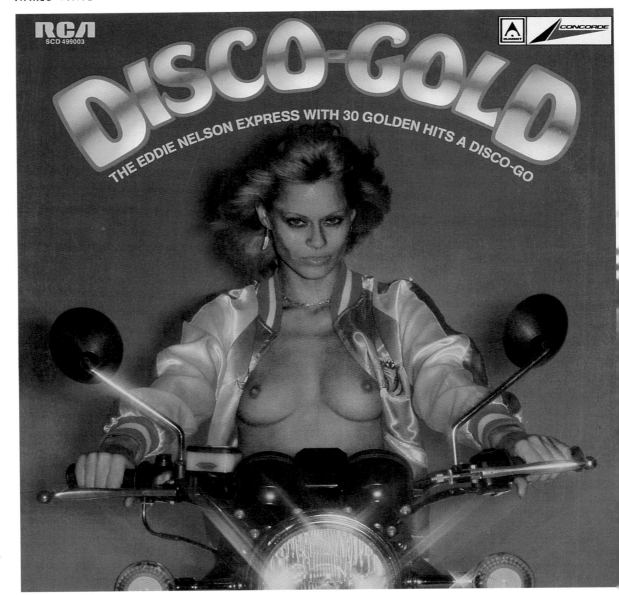

DISCO GOLD
30 GOLDEN HITS A DISCO-GO

THE EDDIE NELSON EXPRESS

SUMMIT · CONCORDE

SIDE 1.

MEDLEY 1

DO YOU REMEMBER (0:31)
(E. Ouwens)

(I Can't Get No) SATISFACTION (1:22)
(Jagger/Richard)

PROUD MARY (1:25)
(J. Fogerty)

AMEN (0:46)
(O. Redding)

MEDLEY 2

FIRE (1:15)
(A. Brown/V. Crane)

SUGAR, SUGAR (0:48)
(Barry/Kim)

BEND ME, SHAPE ME (1:12)
(S. English/L. Weiss)

WOOLY BULLY (1:44)
(D. Samudio)

MEDLEY 3

SHAME AND SCANDALL IN THE FAMILY (1:26)
(Donaldson/Brown)

MONDAY, MONDAY (1:23)
(J. Phillips)

SPANISH HARLEM (1:59)
(J. Leiber/P. Spector)

MEDLEY 4

BLACK IS BLACK (1:43)
(S. Wadey/T. Hayes/M. Grainger)

PRETTY WOMAN (1:30)
(R. Orbison/B. Dees)

MR. TAMBOURINE MAN (1:47)
(B. Dylan)

I PUT A SPELL ON YOU (1:12)
(Trad./arr.: S. Lokhin)

THE BEAT GOES ON (1:53)
(S. Bono)

THE EDDIE NELSON EXPRESS

produced by Eddy Ouwens
recorded at Musicland Studio's, München
(Germany)
medley 1, 2, 3 arranged by Paul Natte
medley 4 arranged by Stan Lokhin

SIDE 2.

MEDLEY 1

DO YOU REMEMBER (0:30)
(E. Ouwens)

HELP! (1:13)
(Lennon/McCartney)

SUZIE Q (1:51)
(Hawkins/Lewis/Broadwater)

LET'S SPEND THE NIGHT TOGETHER (1:30)
(Jagger/Richard)

MEDLEY 2

DANCE INTRODUCTION (1:03)
(J. Rietman/E. Ouwens)

DO YOU WANNA DANCE? (1:06)
(R. Freeman)

LET'S TWIST AGAIN (1:43)
(K. Mann/D. Appel)

THE LOCOMOTION (1:18)
(G. Goffin/C. King)

MEDLEY 3

SUMMER IN THE CITY (1:18)
(J. Sebastian/S. Boone/M. Sebastian)

LADY MARMELADE (Voulez-Vous Coucher Avec Moi, Ce Soir?) (0:46)
(B. Crewe/K. Nolan)

A WHITER SHADE OF PALE (1:14)
(G. Brooker/K. Reid)

JE T'AIME ... MOI NON PLUS (1:37)
(S. Gainsbourg)

MEDLEY 4

YUMMY, YUMMY, YUMMY (1:21)
(A. Resnick/J. Levine)

IN THE YEAR 2525 (1:07)
(R. Evans)

SAVE THE LAST DANCE FOR ME (0:46)
(D. Pomus/M. Shuman)

BYE BYE LOVE (2:00)
(B. Bryant/F. Bryant)

THE EDDIE NELSON EXPRESS

produced by Eddy Ouwens
recorded at Musicland Studio's, München
(Germany)
medley 1, 4 arranged by Hans Hollestelle
medley 2 arranged by Jan Rietman
medley 3 arranged by Stan Lokhin

YAMAHA

 Distributed by
SUMMIT RECORDS PTY. LTD.
176 South Creek Road, Dee Why West 2099, N.S.W. Australia.

Bawdy Party Songs

Not to be outdone by its bigger neighbour, New Zealand got in on the naked act with the pleasant charms of this Kiwi girl-next-door. John Currie "with chorus & party" serve up their offering of Bawdy Party Songs – "The Canine Catastrophe", "Oh Sir Jasper", and "Seven Drunken Nights" set the tone. We must thank our lucky stars that we didn't buy any of the label's other adult offerings, such as the classic *Medical Students Sing Rugby Songs*, or any works by the illustrious Jock Strapp Ensemble.

Bawdy Party Songs is a throwback to the '50s American tradition of rude songs fronted by ruder covers, and what better way to showcase your country's talents than with this delectable young woman – we'll be in Auckland by the time you read this.

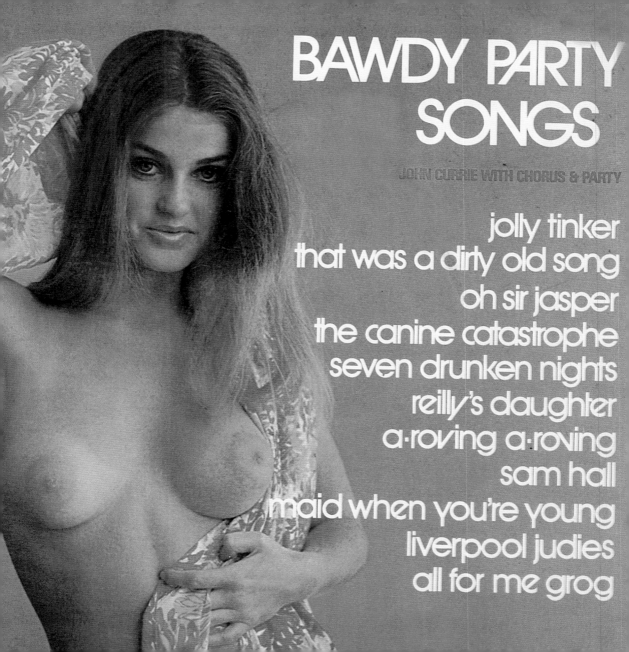

BAWDY PARTY SONGS

JOHN CURRIE WITH CHORUS & PARTY

jolly tinker
that was a dirty old song
oh sir jasper
the canine catastrophe
seven drunken nights
reilly's daughter
a·roving a·roving
sam hall
maid when you're young
liverpool judies
all for me grog

Sexy Songs

New Zealand again, although this time our lovely in the leopardskin briefs has a touch more animal magnetism. No longer the Kiwi girl next door, she's a prowling pussy, a cheetah in her lair on the lookout for her next helping of fresh meat. Meeeooww! Handle with care – this kitten is liable to bite.

The "X Rated Sexational" album features more rude songs, such as the bold "I Wouldn't Say No To A Naughty", the romantic "What Did You Think I Was Going to Say", and the ever-so-subtle "The One-Eyed Trouser Snake". They are sung by one Johnny Logan, but it is definitely not the Irish Eurovision Song Contest winner in another life.

The Perfumed Garden

With **The Perfumed Garden** we have soft-porn for steamy nights with a dramatization of an Arabian story that was written "under pain of death" by Sheikh Nefzawi in the 16th century – "one of the world's most exotic books dedicated to sexual happiness". The cover and Side One's "The Garden of Delights" almost say it all.

The Perfumed Garden dwells on sexual experience in a mystical and philosophical way. It begins with the strains of Arabic music and we are made aware by our female host that "men cannot help falling in love with beautiful women". She is also thankful that men cannot "escape the desire to possess them however hard they try" and to aid us in our erotic quest we are taught the secrets of desire. What then are these secrets? Well, according to Nefzawi we should tease our love with kisses and caresses until her breathing shortens and she begins to sigh and then – and only then – do we move in to provide "the greatest enjoyment she can ever experience".

Our Aussie stunner on the cover seems to be firmly in control, but perhaps she is poised in preparation for, as the Sheikh so poetically puts it, the enjoyment of "the beautiful calm after the most exciting storm".

THE PERFUMED GARDEN

MARION REED'S SPECIAL
STEREO DRAMATISATION
OF THE 16th CENTURY
ARABIAN WORK BY THE
SHEIKH NEFZAWI

MUSIC WORLD

2 RECORD SET

Fanny Hill

Australians certainly like their classic literature, and this time they bring us the masterpiece of erotica, John Cleland's *Fanny Hill* – the tale of a young girl's adventures as she is "seduced, used, and abused in her upward progress through the society of the day".

Our heroine Fanny is orphaned at the tender age of 14, when her erotic story begins. "Poor Fanny, I'm sure I don't know what will become of her" laments a sympathetic friend when Fanny is bundled off to London. "They do say the streets be paved with gold", but upon her arrival Fanny is set to find out the reality amid the lodgings of a brothel.

There follows the story of Fanny's "ride" through society, and the experiences, both painful and pleasant, that unfold on her journey of sexual awakening. Ultimately, Fanny's voyage of discovery is a success and by the time she is 19 she has slept her way to the top and has become a "lady of position and fortune, with a carriage and four". Fanny's "sparkling innocence" remains intact and true love does indeed conquer all – amusing, erotic, and explicit, *Fanny Hill* is also a thoroughly moral tale.

FANNY HILL
•MEMOIRS OF A WOMAN OF PLEASURE!•

$5.49

2 ALBUMS FOR THE
PRICE OF 1

MARION REED'S
SPECIAL STEREO
DRAMATISATION OF
THE 19th CENTURY
WORK BY
JOHN CLELAND

MUSIC WORLD

2
RECORD
SET

Right: *Companion* offers a
demonstration of cover art displaying
its futuristic credentials by launching
itself into space. It looks wonderful
up there, you can see now why they
made all that effort to get to the moon.

COMPANION

PRODUCED BY
BORIS MIDNEY

The Italian Stallions

Amid the ancient Italian landscape, where the vine and olive tree thrive, the culture of modern man has effortlessly embraced fashion, fast cars, and beautiful women. It was in this happy and prosperous terrain that two saxophonists found fame and fortune – and '70s naked vinyl found a new home. Fausto Papetti and Gil Ventura were the men of the moment, bringing the world saxophone-led, easy-listening cover versions fronted by a series of classic nude covers that presented the "*bella figura*" in an inviting, sun-drenched Mediterranean setting.

Fausto Papetti was a master of his art and the star of this blockbuster decade of naked vinyl. He created the "Raccoltas" – a series of records that gave Italy more sax and sex than a Soho jazz club. Released on the Milan-based Durium label, Papetti's phenomenal output consisted of instrumental interpretations of popular classics rendered in a late-night, sultry sax style. In fact, he reworked the better part of the entire international hit parade, creating music that "millions of Italians have… made love to".

Gil Ventura had a similar style to Papetti. His epic-operatic brand of Italian saxophone magic embraced disco and '70s pop to create an upbeat funky melange that provided a sensual musical backdrop to everyday Italian life. Ventura's speciality was a sax-pop cocktail that crammed as many songs as possible into momentous discofied medleys, and what the medleys lacked in artistic credibility, they more than made up for in name-that-tune-ability.

Ventura and Papetti were incredibly successful, and by assimilating and regurgitating the fashions of the era – the catwalk model, the lifestyle magazines, the beach-babe chic – they sold countless records and left us the legacy of a seemingly endless range of memorable nude covers.

The two Italian artistes continued their craft well into

"Fausto Papetti was a master of his art and the star of this blockbuster decade of naked vinyl'"

the '80s. On Papetti's death in 1999, he was said, in understated terms, to have left "a small but unfillable void" in the world of Italian "la musica leggara". The duo's records and accompanying covers stand testament to the fact that Italians can, along with a passion for beauty, fashion, music, and wine, always find time for love and a little dessert.

"...music that 'millions of Italians ...have made love to'"

18a Raccolta

Fausto Papetti released a seemingly endless series of sax-based albums and decorated them with a series of the most amazingly beautiful Italian women. We have chosen the best for your delectation and by so doing hopefully Fausto's star will once again rise. To Fausto and his legacy of album cover art, we say "*grazie mille*". This Italian classic, *18a Raccolta*, shows that the sophisticated styling of Ferrari is for once matched by nature's handiwork.

Pages 228-29: Fausto is at it again with what you might call his "playful porn" on *21a Raccolta* and *22a Raccolta*. From the days when smoking was still sexy, we have a model who wouldn't look out of place on the cover of *Vogue*, with clothes on of course, while down on the beach there is a Mediterranean beach study clad loosely in denim.

FAUSTO PAPETTI

18ª

RACCOLTA

SAX

ms AI 77342

DURIUM

STEREOFONICO
compatibile

SOLEA
A BLUE SHADO
THE WAY WE WE
L'ULTIMA NEVE DI PRIMAVER
GESM
LOVE'S THE

PECCATO VENIA
TENTATIO
NUTBUSH CITY LIMI
DELITTO DI REGIN
RICORDO DI LIL
THE WINDMILLS OF YOUR MIN

FAUSTO PAPETTI sax

MONO - STEREO

DURIUM

ms AI 77371

21ª raccolta

MONO - STEREO
DURIUM
ms AI 77380

FaustoPapetti
SAX

22ª RACCOLTA

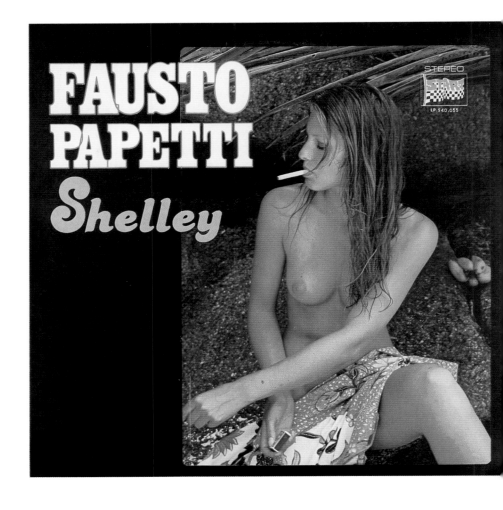

FAUSTO
PAPETTI
Shelley

STEREO

LP.540.055

Above + right: Here we have two more
Fausto specials. *Santo Domingo* is the
height of Faust Papetti's musical majesty
and his funky Italian brand of "la musica
leggera" is here aptly displayed on
"Facciata B" with an epic drum-led
cover of the song "Sweet Charity".

FAUSTO PAPETTI

sax

Santo Domingo

stereo
START

Sax Club Nr 16

Gil Ventura is the second member of the "Italian stallions" and on *Sax Club Nr 16* he offers us more sax-based tunes, along with a cover hot enough to melt the vinyl. In this provocative image, our leading lady may be constrained, but she turns the tables by coolly staring down at us dismissively, begging the question, who's really in control?

The album also features a cover version of the soundtrack to *Bilitis*, which means that for once the cover art reflected the musical product.

3C 054-18297

STEREO

GIL VENTURA

BILITIS
GUERRE STELLARI
AGENTE 007, LA SPIA CHE MI AMAVA
I FEEL LOVE
NON MI LASCIARE
ZODIACS
MOON FLOWER
MARIA ELENA

SAX CLUB Nr ⓰

LA PANTERA ROSA
THRILLER
NEW YORK, NEW YORK
TOMORROW
DON'T LET ME BE MISUNDERSTOOD

Running

Trapeze offer us a classy piece of '70s Brit rock along with a super-sexy interpretation of athletic female movement. The album was released in the late '70s and offers a few clues that we're creeping towards a new decade with the pocket calculator typography and slick photography.

Though Trapeze didn't really go the distance in the fame stakes, this effort shows that they most definitely had stamina for the rock lifestyle. The cover's busty blonde also stakes a claim for a little vinyl fame and we think she's got the moves to match the rock grooves.

Released on Shark Records, *Running* brings the '70s to a close with a burst of colour and sexy design. It's a fitting finale to a decade that saw sexy imagery go fully mainstream. And as *Naked Vinyl* covers the erotic miles, we can think back and remember a decade of laid-back sexual expression.

Fausto Papetti
27ª Raccolta

STER
DURIUM
ms Al 7"

4

The '80s:
Sex is a Four-Letter Word

Richard Strauss

In the '80s even classical music, surely one of the last artistic bastions of conservative taste, went erotic – and it certainly had the raw materials to explore, as Richard Strauss demonstrated with finesse in an album themed around his erotic masterpiece on the second side, "Dance of the Seven Veils". For those few pop-lovers lacking the essential points of cultural reference, "Don Juan" is to the licentious domain of the lothario what The Beatles are to rock quartets – in other words, with few peers; meanwhile the dance is a reference to the corrupt temptress Salome's erotically provocative performance at the court of King Herod. Salome's idea of "good head" was that of the one belonging to John the Baptist, served to her on a platter. And if she looked like this album cover image, it was small wonder that King Herod could not resist delivering on his promise.

RICHARD STRAUSS
DANCE OF THE SEVEN VEILS
DON JUAN · TILL EULENSPIEGEL
DEATH AND TRANSFIGURATION

RUDOLF KEMPE
Dresden State Orchestra

EMI

HIS MASTER'S VOICE

HMV
Greensleeve

Horizontal Refreshment

Supercharge here make their second appearance in *Naked Vinyl*, courtesy of another slice of classic Aussie rock and an '80's-styled cover that captures a little of the decade's design aesthetic. As for the title, well *Horizontal Refreshment* surely takes equal top-spot with bedroom gymnastics in the league table of sexual euphemisms.

As the cover's neon-lit sexy lady quenches her thirst, we think it's time to put the case forward for the curly straw revival. Has there ever been a better or more stylish way to enjoy a drink? Has the childhood joy of sucking a coloured fruity drink all the way to the top then letting it slide back into glass ever been bettered? We don't think so. And while we're on the subject, how about day-glo jumpers? And what about those hats you can drink from? Then again ...

All in all though, surely such a creative and colourful decade deserves a bit more aesthetic credit. But then we're biased – we did so love those straws.

27a Raccolta

Fausto's at it again with a golden lady enjoying the pleasures of childish pastimes in an entirely adult way. Fausto Papetti's *Raccolta* series spanned three decades and ran to over 50 editions, until he finally tired of its erotic charms. He was one of the few naked vinyl artists who made it through to the age of the CD and it says much about his striking sexual imagery that it survived this change to the compact era.

On *27a Raccolta,* Fausto gives us a couple of his own compositions – "Lovers" and "Orange" – along with covers of "Miss You" a Jagger/Richards composition and a medley based around the movie *Grease.* The medley contains the classic Barry Gibb-composed theme song, originally sung by Frankie Valli, along with the instrumental "Alone at the Drive-In Movie" and the epic Travolta/Newton-John-sung number, "You're the One that I Want".

This time round they get the Fausto Papetti instrumental sax interpretation, while we're just happy to have mentioned a classic sexy movie like *Grease* within the pages of *Naked Vinyl.*

Fausto Papetti
27ª Raccolta

STEREO
DURIUM 33
ms AI 77401

35a Raccolta

Fausto Papetti strolls on with *35a Raccolta*, whose cover art places us firmly in time and place: a slender model sporting a Walkman amid a spray of lurid colour, exemplifying all we need to know about what passed for style during the '80s.

The album includes "My One and Only Love" and this might be the reason Fausto gives for playing, but who or what is his first love? It might be a string of sun-bleached joggers, or it could be his mother or his sax. Sadly, we will never know, but in keeping with the sentiments of the great Barry White's "You're the First, the Last, My Everything", it may well have been his music.

Our first love is this shiny yellow and green cover and the sexy and shy model that graces its exterior. We're not ashamed to admit a certain fondness for '80s stylings and this cover encapsulates all we love about that decadent decade.

FAUSTO PAPETTI

35ª

RACCOLTA

MY ONE
AND ONLY LOVE

Sex Goes Pop

Passion in the '80s was a strange business. Just as we began to enjoy the freedom to do what comes naturally, without the censorship of social disapproval, the door marked "sexual liberty" was once more shut in our overheated faces. The licence afforded by the sexual revolution was suddenly haunted by the spectre of AIDs, in response to which a more conservative social agenda sought to reaffirm "traditional" values in opposition to the culture of sexual freedom.

As a consequence, sex became a subject to be handled safely, and the media and the entertainment industry served up slices of erotic pie to us in such small portions that our appetites were never quite sated. While some pop artists railed against the climate of sexual censorship, such as Frankie Goes to Hollywood with "Relax", many others lent their weight to those advocating that people literally play it safe. Boy George represented the less sex-obsessed ordinary folk when

he famously said that he would rather have a nice cup of tea – very British.

Meanwhile, in the actual Hollywood of Los Angeles, during the '80s sex came a distant second to the big-budget thrills and spills of the action movie genre, as audiences were bombarded with the gung-ho violent technological terminations of Rambo and Arnie, who showed us graphically how they managed to work up a sweat. If any sex did come along, it tended to be slushy and sentimental, such as *An Officer And A Gentleman*, or downright scary, *Fatal Attraction*-style. The alternative was the breasts-and-booze slapstick soft porn of Porkies or the frat-pack naughtiness of Animal House and its ilk. All in all, the '80s were about guns 'n' girls and toys for the boys – and the bare torsos on view were male and glistening.

Album cover art was enveloped in this tidal wave of sexual timidity and our gaze was even temporarily averted

"Relax, don't do it, when you want to come" Frankie Goes to Hollywood

from the cover image by the introduction of new playback technology in the form of a shiny silver compact disc, which looked cool and came accompanied by a minimalist design aesthetic. But in the end, though, it was sex itself that proved it had staying power and what many craved the most was put back on the musical map by the full-steam-ahead nudity of Madonna's *Erotica* and the misogyny of hip-hop. Soon television was awash with what just decades earlier had been attacked as "pornography" – eventually, even porn itself became mainstream and sex these days rears its naughty head just about everywhere.

Many have now fallen in love again with the '80s, but perhaps we should look back and remember that the sexual latitude that exists today wasn't necessarily born of lip-gloss and odd, albeit amusing, headgear.

In the '80s, sex was most definitely a four-letter word.

Medley in Sax

Fausto seemed to go on forever – "non stop" he would have us believe. With this offering he brings us the chic of '80s style, the superslim model in black high heels representing the ultimate yuppie fantasy.

You should have noticed by now how the ideal of beauty has changed over the decades, from the fulsome female figures of the '50s and '60s to the pencil-thin supermodels who have held sway until the present. By the '80s, breasts had been replaced by beauty as a model's prime asset. Having covered quite a distance on practically the one tank of fuel, Fausto probably deserves some sort of credit for the longevity of his performance, but perhaps including a cover version of "Do You Really Want to Hurt Me?" is pushing his luck just a bit too far?

As this is our last Fausto Papetti masterpiece, we have to ask: "Ti e piaciuoto" (Was it good for you?).

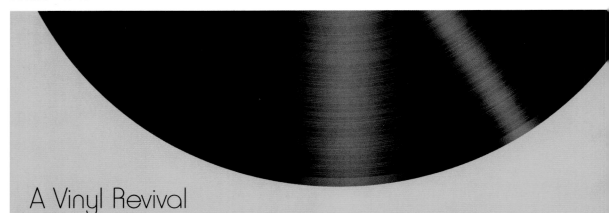

A Vinyl Revival

In the early '90s, as far as many people were concerned, vinyl was all but dead and buried. Vinyl was out on its ear thanks to two love affairs, one being that of the record companies' with CDs and the other the public's with innovation. Who could really have been surprised that something so relatively heavy and cumbersome, which warps, scratches and has to be turned over halfway through playing, had met a natural end? But, strangely, many people continued to love the look and feel of records – both for their sound and size, as well as for the pictures on their sleeves. Records reminded us of our youth; they were toys for adults to play with without fear of embarrassment. Most of us can remember the first vinyl single we bought, but how many of us can remember our first CD?

Vinyl was effectively saved by the demand of DJs for the large-format single, which was an essential tool of their trade. The 12-inch single was practically irreplaceable and it remains to this day the best mechanism for keeping clubs bopping. While some people were filling charity shops with their out-of-date record collections, a mini vinyl revival was taking place. With the 12-inch single maintaining sales and momentum, other forms of vinyl reasserted their respective claims to a renewed musical existence. The "remix" was king for a day; the "limited edition" was the record labels' preferred format; the "bootleg" brought us hard-to-find rare grooves along with, for a time at least, bizarre juxtapositions of competing tunes; while the "reissue" once more allowed popularized albums to be released both legally and illegally. Even the ungainly 10-inch had a comeback of sorts, while increasing numbers of new releases included a vinyl

"Vinyl was effectively saved by the demand of DJs for the large format single which was an essential tool of their trade"

counterpart, often with added extras to make them that much more collectable. Vinyl's market share has bounced back and the old-fashioned yet unbeatable record disc looks set to be around for a lot longer.

The return of vinyl as a force to be reckoned with has been accompanied by a renaissance of the nude cover. Swept up in our love of all things retro, musical forms as diverse as hip-hop, easy-listening and house have plundered the nude cover's stylistic kudos. Hip-hop has always been the most sexist of music forms and its covers have reflected this, while house, in its more glamourous and knowingly sexy way, has consistently embraced nudity. The easy-listening, lounge-core revival, which has plundered the imagery and sexual ethos of the '60s, also took naked vinyl to its heart and the nude cover is as ubiquitous today as it has ever been.

Hawaï: mélodies des îles

One theme that will by now have become apparent to readers is the ongoing love affair with Hawaii. Album cover art returned time and again to the islanders' culture and music, not to mention the charms of her comely hula girls.

This French album by Orchestre Daikiki is a collection of "magical Hawaiian guitar", but for most red-blooded males what engages our interest is less the thought or sounds of guitars than of the Hawaiian girls.

As we admire the combination of beach, weather, and trees, and almost breathe in the atmosphere of the picture-postcard scene of perfection, we cannot help but gaze enraptured at the all-too-obvious attractions of our long-tressed Hawaiian babe and allow our imaginations to drift, slowly transforming ourselves into an erect palm tree whose trunk is being caressed gently in the bathing glow of the warm sunshine. Sheer bliss.

Guitare Hawaïenne

The long fascination that Westerners have had for the islands of the Pacific can be explained by a potent cocktail whose ingredients are natural beauty – of both the surroundings and the inhabitants – and the native peoples' culturally liberal attitude to sex. In the 18th and 19th centuries islands such as Tahiti were much sought-after stopovers for sailors, who spoke of them as paradises of sensual gratification. Sexual hospitality played a central role in the famous episode of the mutiny aboard Captain Bligh's *Bounty* – how many schoolboys could fail to have etched into their memories some of those celluloid scenes of passion they witnessed on television? And we're not thinking of Marlon Brando.

We close now with this sublime example of Hawaiian styling. You can see why Fletcher Christian and his crewmates didn't fancy the journey back to England!

GUITARE HAWAÏENNE

Jean Hemmer

ALOHA OE
LA GUITARE ET LA MER
SUR LA PLAGE DE WAIKIKI
LE BATEAU DES ILES
FLORIDA
VAHINÉ
LE BATEAU DE TAHITI...

DOUBLE ALBUM

CARRERE

Acknowledgements

Thanks to: Mike and Christine, Mum and Dad, Kate and Woody; Tristan Manco, the Savage-Jones Clan; Eduard at Normal Records, Andrea Grimes at SFPL, Malcolm Pearce at Damont Audio; O'Brien's, Hyams' and Bloom's; Mark for Niagra; Jo and Will and Chris and Paul; Nicki Ratcliffe at EMI; Betsy Brown at WEA; The Rev. Warren Debenham; Winter and Casey; Martin Combeer, Pursuit Internet and Blow Up; all at Repsycho; Wanda McSwain at Elektra; Preston Peek at Vinyllives and Tony Wilds at Wildsscene; all in Japan, Bristol, Brighton, Weston, London; and anyone we've forgotten.

Bibliography

That's Sexploitation
Eddie Muller and Daniel Faris/Titan books/1997
The Essential Lenny Bruce
edited by John Cohen/Panther/1975
Last Night A DJ Saved My Life
Bill Brewster and Frank Broughton/Headline/1999

The Big Book of Filth
Jonathon Green/Cassell/2001
The Lonely Planet Italian Phrasebook
Maurice Riverso/Lonely Planet/1998
**Various back issues of Playboy, Adam,
and Exotica/Et Cetera magazines**

Useful Websites

normal-records.com
vinyllives.com
wildsscene.com
ebay.co.uk

jackdiamond.com
plastic.it
allmusic.com